THE
NAME
CHANGER

The Name Changer: How to Heal From the Devastation of Divorce by Cary Seaholm

All Scripture quotations, unless otherwise indicated, are taken from the Holy Bible, New International Version®, NIV®. Copyright ©1973, 1978, 1984, 2011 by Biblica, Inc.™ Used by permission of Zondervan. All rights reserved worldwide. www.zondervan.com The "NIV" and "New International Version" are trademarks registered in the United States Patent and Trademark Office by Biblica, Inc.™

Published by CHOSEN Counseling Services
ISBN: 979-8-9872216-0-0 (paperback), 979-8-9872216-1-7 (epub)

Publishing and Design Services: MelindaMartin.me

THE
NAME
CHANGER

HOW TO HEAL FROM
THE DEVASTATION OF DIVORCE

CARY SEAHOLM, LCSW

I dedicate this book to
My Forever Love, Jesus,
and to my favorite people in the world,
Trey, Carisia, Cassandra, and Joshua.

I love you.

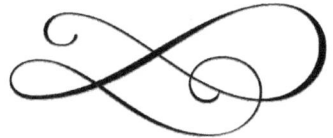

CONTENTS

Separation and divorce result in bone-crushing loneliness. Readers will learn how to face the vulnerability of desire and temptation. They will identify their triggers and understand that although our feelings may be intense, they do not dictate our holiness.

The Word of God is clear: in order to be forgiven, we must forgive. The importance and benefits of forgiveness are found in exploring the following questions: How does one cope with feelings of anger? Is forgiveness a one-time event? How do you forgive someone who purposely wants to harm you? What happens when that person continues to hurt you?

Forgiveness is a choice. Purity of heart is an action, encompassing our motives and thoughts. Readers are encouraged to move past forgiveness and take the ultimate step in healing by walking in purity of heart toward a former spouse.

Life often seems unfair after a divorce. Others have hope and joy, but we don't. This hopelessness manifests in emotional paralysis and depression. Facing the reality of these feelings can lead to encouragement by choosing to look to the only One who can save.

Most parents would not intentionally inflict harm on their children. However, in divorce, children often suffer most. Practical suggestions and clinical principles are provided, enabling parents to help their children through their own coping and healing processes.

Many enter the divorce process with inaccurate information and unrealistic expectations. Here, information is given to counter the statement, "I wish I would have known then, what I know now," relating to the business side of divorce. Current societal information is offered as a guide to avoid emotional and financial pitfalls during the process.

Words can be sources of healing or pain. When asked about the intimate details of their marriage, some will be loyal and loving while others will depart, often after saying hurtful things. This chapter encourages the reader to follow Jesus' example. He was the perfect listener and in perfect control of his responses. "If it is possible, as far as it depends on you, live at peace with everyone" (Romans 12:18).

God created us to live in relationship. For some, that companionship comes through marriage. However, before this can take place one should go through a process of healing and wholeness. This chapter explores things one should consider before dating again.

God is the redeemer of our past, present, and future. In conclusion, the reader is encouraged to remove the Scarlet Letter of divorce and embrace the letter "C" as Christ is the one who gives us a new identity. Continuing the journey to healing and wholeness, readers will grieve the loss of a "happily ever after." They are encouraged to create new dreams for their future.

INTRODUCTION

I am a Christian woman whose life was shattered by divorce. In the aftermath, while I struggled to put the pieces together, voices—mine and others berated me, "You're not good enough—not good enough to save your marriage, and *definitely* not good enough for God. If you were, the Lord would have intervened and restored your marriage."

He didn't.

Divorce is not only my reality, but that of many Christian women. Despite countless resources, therapy, conferences, and ministry materials—sometimes marriages cannot be saved.

Even though my previous life was destroyed, through God's healing and grace, I have been renewed. The divorce process forced me to grow and stretch while strengthening my faith. I have experienced the all-consuming love of my Heavenly Father throughout my deepest time of need.

I hope to inspire those who have suffered a similar tragic loss. By candidly incorporating parts of my journey, biblical principles, and clinical insight, I want to encourage readers to courageously identify the areas of their lives which need God's transformative, healing touch.

Intense and overwhelming emotions accompany divorce. Anger, disillusionment, hopelessness, and a pervasive sense of failure stalked me. When I acknowledged these and placed them in God's hands, his love overtook me because, *God's love is greater than divorce.*

I want you to be strengthened by each piece of information in this book. I'll be transparent for I've walked this road and made mistakes, but have learned to keep moving forward. Many of us have endured or are enduring similar hardships.

There is hope.

You are not alone.

ONE

The Scarlet Letter

I am a licensed clinical social worker, yet none of my professional experience prepared me for divorce. As a woman of faith, I never imagined that after ten years of marriage I'd be a single mother of three. Labeled with the scarlet letter "D"—divorced.

This invisible mark tethered my life and pierced my heart wherever I went. Simple activities like walking through the mall with my children made me painfully aware of strangers who fixed their gaze on my bare ring finger. Social events stung when I greeted a friend's husband, and she moved closer to him. My stomach churned when a married man stared at me just a bit too long. Unease stiffened conversations and time with friends and family who weighed every word I spoke, eager to find questionable content. I felt like a deer in an open field during hunting season.

In Nathaniel Hawthorne's novel *The Scarlet Letter*, Hester Prynne was sentenced to wear a scarlet letter "A" as a perpetual announcement of her sin of adultery. In her puritanical society, she embodied evil. Scorned and ostracized, she was considered a second-class citizen. Yet, despite this, she became one of the most charitable women in town. Because of her gracious character, newcomers assumed the stitched letter carried a noble significance. Although society branded Hester, she rose above the mark of condemnation, and in the process, transformed it.

Branding occurs in subtle and insidious ways. Without realizing it, we allow labels to define us. Negative ones bind our lives with guilt and shame like ever-tightening cords, strangling our souls, suffocating our identity.

The label "D" of divorce begins with a legal ruling. Yet, before, during, and after that designation is applied, people often judge incorrectly, unaware of the facts. Ill-informed, they assign reasons for our failure. "You didn't satisfy your husband's sexual needs." "You should've cooked more, kept a tidier home, worked more, or worked less." "If you'd taken better care of your appearance, he'd never have looked at anyone else." The underlying message is clear—our efforts, appearance, and character weren't good enough to keep our marriages together.

We failed.

In addition to the invisible, but tangible tags proclaiming our failure, we're viewed as defective and immoral, forcing us to guard ourselves in situations where we used to relax. Friendly behavior is now considered flirty. Although much remains unspoken, we suffer the heat of accusations and suspicions. So, our broken souls are twice violated. First, by the demise of the marriage. Then, by the stigma of divorce.

Failure and Rejection

The decision to divorce was gut-wrenching, I not only feared what others would think, I *felt* like a failure. I fantasized and prayed my husband would wake up one day and realize his mistake. I wanted what well-meaning family and church members predicted would come to pass—restoration. It never happened. He never came back.

Because of my church and educational background, I ignorantly assumed I understood divorce and its components. As a result, I inaccurately judged others, and during my own divorce, I was judged wrongly. Several months into the process, I took off my wedding ring—a huge step. Wearing it sustained my denial, allowing me to cling to the hope our union would be restored.

When I faced the inevitable and removed the outward symbol of my marriage commitment, those closest to me proclaimed their judgment. "If only she had more faith, God would have restored her marriage." They assured me, "God wants to put your marriage back together." They had no idea their words pierced like daggers.

Divorce is my reality, one at odds with my Christian worldview. I struggled with the harm this would inflict on my testimony. What would people think? *Where is her God now? She says she faithfully serves him, so why didn't he rescue her marriage? If this is how Christians live, why would I want what she has?*

I wanted to be salt and light for the Lord, but my life was shattered, and my family was falling apart. I wanted to bring people to Jesus, but my husband left, throwing me away like a piece of garbage. Every negative thought stitched the scarlet letter "D" tighter around my heart. My own judgment provided the inflexible thread that relentlessly tied the knots securing that emblem of failure.

Condemning thoughts overshadowed the truth of my identity in Jesus: God didn't save me only to thrust me into a prison of disapproval. He didn't want me to be bound by the thoughts and opinions of others. Yet, the weight of guilt and shame left me defeated and defensive.

Divorced Christian women get it. We live with a stigma that accompanies the desertion and betrayal by the one we planned to grow old with, whose opinion mattered most. The person who promised to love us in good times and in bad. We understand the pain when tears and prayers end with abandonment.

These words helped me. "The Lord will call you back as if you *were a wife deserted and distressed in spirit—a wife who married young, only to be rejected,'* says your God" (Isaiah 54:6 emphasis added).

Rejection pierces the soul, creating a trauma so pervasive it's difficult to express it to those outside of the situation. This hinders healing. The invisible, but very real scarlet letter, is merely a by-product.

Only God can heal us. He understands our suffering and calls us to leave that prison and walk in his freedom. When Christ came, those he loved most turned away from him, so he understands our anguish. In a small way, our rejection by someone we have loved deeply is like his.

From Rejected to Treasured

In the wake of divorce, many wives are overlooked and treated as second-class citizens. Bystanders, absorbed in their own lives, unwilling to be tainted by association, may distance themselves. In Matthew 15:21–28 a woman came to Jesus on her hands and knees begging for her daughter's healing. At first, Christ ignored her requests and her pleas seemed futile. She persisted. The disciples complained about her, yet she continued. When Christ finally responded, he called her a *dog*.

This insult drew attention to a cultural attitude, testing all who were present. When he ignored her cries for help, no one seemed to care. *Dog* validated the sentiment, she didn't matter.

We can learn so much from her. Instead of quitting, she refused to leave without the help she needed. She took the label and turned it into a living analogy of her status as an expectant beggar at Jesus' feet. This woman knew what she wanted and believed Christ cared enough to heal her daughter. She let *nothing* stand in her way.

Her extraordinary response challenged everyone. Jesus commended her. *"Dear woman, your faith is great. Your request is granted."* He called her *dear*, a remarkable compliment. *He* admired *her* faith and exalted her. In contrast, we can read many places in the gospels where Jesus reprimanded the disciples for their *lack* of faith.

He announced her true worth. Similarly, Christ looks beyond our marital status. In his eyes we discover that divorce *doesn't* make us less valuable. Instead, we're treasured beyond measure by the God of the universe, because of who he is and because he chose to love us.

"Though the mountains be shaken and the hills be removed, yet my unfailing love for you will not be shaken nor my covenant of peace be removed,' says the LORD, who has compassion on you" (Isaiah 54:10).

Divorce shakes our world. Security collapses. The future looks bleak. However, even when we don't see or feel it, God's love for us is fully intact. *Our marital status doesn't alter his love for us.*

We succumb to wavering emotions and accept the scarlet letter's lies. We allow other people or organizations to pin that insidious letter on our chest. Or, even worse, we pin the guilty letter on ourselves. How can we tear the scarlet letter of reproach from our lives? How can we heal when we doubt our self-worth or allow the cloud of stigma to follow us? Can we rip it off without leaving deep scars?

We all bear invisible brands. If not divorce, it may be shameful choices that mar our self-image such as— "A" for abortion, addiction, adulterer, and "C" for criminal. But whatever the label, Christ assures us that we are new creatures for the old has passed away and we are made new (2 Corinthians 5:17). His label covers our old ones, just as his power breaks our captivity. We must believe this in order to relinquish our guilt, step out of our invisible prison, and embrace the future God has for us.

Tearing Apart the Scarlet Letter

Jesus invites us to take many steps to tear apart this scarlet letter.

He frees us from our faulty thinking and the opinions of others when we immerse ourselves in his Word. Each of us is a person of worth despite the difficulties we face. Remembering this is harder during the transition from married to single. Because we can't check the box for single or married, we're in limbo travelling through two worlds and working through the kinks of our new life. However, despite the disapproval of others, we can walk in the Lord's power and liberation, free to reject the judgements of others.

We stop saying divorcee. Our marital status does *not* define us. My "ex-husband" has a name. If I don't want to refer to him by name, I can call him the "father of my children." I don't have to call him "my ex" for the rest of my life. When we ended the marriage, we chose separate lives. I don't have to continue to identify myself in terms of him.

We consciously let go of the guilt and shame of divorce. When we choose to forgive ourselves, we can learn from our mistakes and grow. Only we know what took place behind the closed doors of our home and what we did to heal or destroy the union. If we need forgiveness, we should ask for it.

Finally, and most importantly, we seek God, not just in the fresh days and weeks of grief, but as a lifestyle. The Bible is filled with promises of God's love, care, and affirmation of us. Because he knows everything, we can approach him with total transparency, telling him about our sadness, anger, and worries. God alone can affirm our true worth for he sees us not only as we are now, but as he created us to be.

> " . . . so that Christ may dwell in your hearts through faith. And I pray that you, being rooted and established in love, may have power, together with all the Lord's holy people, to grasp how wide and long and high and deep is the love of Christ, and to know this love that surpasses knowledge—that you may be filled to the measure of all the fullness of God" (Ephesians 3:17–19).

Remove shame and replace it with the
blood-stained letter C for Christ.

TESTIMONY: LORI HUDSON,
MARRIED FOR THIRTEEN YEARS AFTER TWO DIVORCES

I have been divorced not once, but twice. Although I've been remarried for thirteen years, I still feel people see the "D" on my forehead. After my second divorce, many people quit talking to me and ignored me. The silence that hurt most was from my father. When I told my dad I was divorcing for the second time, his disgust was palpable. He didn't speak to me for over a year. I was alone, vulnerable, and needed him, but during my crisis, he turned his back on me.

Few people cared enough to even ask if I was okay. However, some very sweet people in my church supported and accepted me. In fact, if not for them, I don't think I would have made it through the crippling cloud of despair. A few years later, I decided those who shut me out weren't worth my time, and now I feel sorry for their shallowness.

People have misconstrued my motives. I still sense an uneasiness from some wives when I speak to their husbands, so I never talk alone with a man. If I have to address a man, I make sure my husband is present.

One uncomfortable situation occurred after my second divorce. My youngest daughter who was in 4-H club was raising a heifer and sheep and I needed assistance to hook up a trailer for the animals. Another 4-H family down the road from us had a teenage son a little older than my daughter. I called and asked if someone could help us. The mom agreed but didn't specify when they could come.

Early the next morning, the mom and her son knocked on my door. Because I wasn't expecting them, I answered in my granny style thick blue robe.

When the mom saw me, she said, "Oh my," and acted nervous.

I said, "I'll be right out."

They said, "Okay," and soon the trailer was hooked up. I thanked them and went about my day.

A week later, a mutual friend called and said my behavior was inappropriate and questioned "How dare I try to seduce that boy."

Shocked and speechless, I couldn't even fathom her accusation. I told her no such thing had even entered my mind.

She said, "Well, it didn't appear that way."

I couldn't understand how anyone would think that about me.

Thankfully, my wonderful pastor provided me with good biblical counsel after my second divorce. Both were extremely difficult, and I have cried my share of tears. In those times when I called out to God, I have felt his presence. He has loved and comforted me. Additionally, he brought good people into my life who have provided a listening ear and even a laugh or two along the way.

Removing the scarlet letter is the first step in no longer allowing our circumstances and the opinions of others to gain a stranglehold over our lives and future. Christ came to heal, not to condemn. He is our healer and our value and identity come from him.

Christ gives us a new name:
BELOVED.

CHAPTER ONE: THE SCARLET LETTER

Prayer

Lord, I thank you because your Word says that anyone who is in Christ is a new creation; old things have passed away and all things have become new (Isaiah 43:18–19) and there is no condemnation for those who are in Christ Jesus (Romans 8:1). I hold on to those promises and choose to release the guilt and shame of my past. I know you love me, and nothing can separate me from your love. Help me walk through the healing you have for me. I know you have a good future and a good hope for me (Jeremiah 29:11).

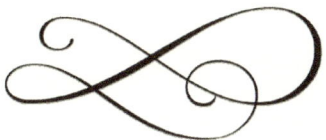

The Lord makes firm
the steps of the one who delights in him;
though he may stumble, he will not fall,
for the Lord upholds him with his hand.

—*Psalm 37:23–24*

Reflection

Before answering these questions, ask the Holy Spirit to bring to mind the areas of your life addressed in this chapter which need healing and change.

1. When have you felt judged incorrectly because you're divorced or going through a divorce? How has this affected your self-worth?

2. Do you feel guarded and fearful someone will misconstrue your motives? How have you handled this?

3. How do you refer to your former spouse? If it has a negative connotation, how could you change it?

TWO

Grieving the Loss

Divorce is a death. Gone are the dreams of growing old with the one person you vowed to love for all time. Describing the emotions surrounding divorce is difficult because starting over isn't a single event. The process begins with turmoil, continues through separation, and culminates long after the ink is dry on the final decree.

When I told a friend about my divorce, she lamented that hers had been worse than cancer. I was taken aback to think that after her horrific health battle, she rated divorce as a worse experience. Her stark words revealed the devastation that surrounds the demise of a marriage. Only those who have experienced it can attest to its agony.

One of the greatest contributions to understanding how people cope with sorrow is in Elisabeth Kübler-Ross's 1969 book *On Death and Dying* where she describes the five stages of grief: denial, anger, bargaining, depression, and acceptance. These can also be translated into how we grieve the loss of a marriage. These stages don't occur in a particular order, and one can vacillate between any of them at any time. We all grieve differently, so it's good to have a basic understanding of this process in order to gain insight and normalize our own reactions.

Denial

Denial can be an effective coping mechanism for a brief time. It buffers the initial shock of a situation and allows us to begin the process of coming to terms with what is happening. A brief time in this stage can help reestablish balance.

Because the toxicity of my relationship developed slowly, I viewed certain behaviors as normal. I didn't grasp the extent of our dysfunction until the bomb of reality exploded. I was blind to the truth—I lived with a stranger. The same person I shared the intimate details of my life with and trusted was unrecognizable. I had no idea what he was capable of. This revelation shattered my life, leaving me filled with dread and anxiety about the future.

My first moments in survival mode, trying to stabilize the situation, masked the magnitude of my pain. God, in his mercy, poured a spiritual Novocain over my heart that enabled me to cope. However, my numbness caused a false sense of security and I irresponsibly considered dating. Looking back, I realize that premature decision would have added more destruction to an already difficult situation. I needed to be whole before I thought about another committed relationship.

Anger

When someone emerges from the haze of denial, anger rears its ugly head. For me, numbness gave way to debilitating rage. Fury surged at how much of my life I'd invested in my husband and how his selfish actions wounded and destroyed me. I was indignant over losing my family and resented the difficulties my children would encounter. Each new piece of information about his hidden life fueled the flames of resentment at the injustice of it all.

This part of the process was the most difficult as I struggled to control my intense reactions and feelings. During this time, I knew any interaction with him wouldn't end well. My unrelenting desire for revenge blocked my ability to think clearly. I wanted him to hurt. At times I called only to scream at him. I even mailed him a package of our professional wedding pictures in shreds.

None of this quenched my rage. Worse yet, he didn't seem to care, going about making a new life and doing as he pleased without any visible remorse. All the while, I carried the responsibility of caring for our children while my world collapsed. Thoughts flooded my mind. *How am I going to do this? Will I ever love again? What man will want a woman with three kids?*

Writing poetry offered a much-needed release for my pain.

To My Alleged Love

I gave you all my love and you repaid me with betrayal.
You treated me with disdain and mocked my affections,
Never enough, my kindness rebuffed.
I cried out to you, pleading for your love.
My cries fell on deaf ears.
Now you wonder why I'm free;
Now you wonder where I will go from here;
Liberated from the life sentence of your reproach.
How you have scarred me.
Made me jaded and untrusting of love,
The very thing I dreamed of.
Instead of a dream, I lived my worst nightmare.
The very thing I feared, I have become.
A woman scorned, trying to win the love of her betrayer.

Best Time of Our Lives

Mourning the life I thought we had,
Grieving all the wasted effort,
The love I wished to possess was never mine.
So many lies;
And now you want to reminisce about the "best times of our lives."
Put on the rose-colored lens I used to wear-
Not wanting to face the reality of your perpetual schemes,
The life I fought so hard for,
The abuse I endured,

Neglected and abandoned by you.
How could you expect me to believe you ever loved me?
Our life has been a lie.
When the verbal assaults came "At least he is faithful," I would say,
Those endless nights I cried myself to sleep, believing it was me
Believing the lie that I was to blame,
Trying desperately to hold on to something that was poisoning my mind
Killing me softly on the inside.
The truth shall set you free, the Bible says.
The prison doors are finally open, and I'd be a fool to step back in.

I've met many women who years after their divorces still carry unresolved negative feelings for their former husbands. Although they may have established new relationships, hatred still simmers below the surface, affecting every part of their lives.

I related to these bitter women during my turmoil. I didn't want to face my feelings because I thought it made me less Christian to be *this* angry. Meanwhile, the mounting frustration bubbled over. Because I was easily irritated and overwhelmed, there were times I treated my children harshly, which I deeply regret.

I also withdrew emotionally from others. I had nothing to give. Everywhere I went there were constant reminders of my broken family pulling at my emotions. I wasn't outwardly hostile, but I carried a deep resentment at my own isolation.

The Bible doesn't say all anger is sinful but warns us about holding on to it. "In your anger do not sin. Do not let the sun go down while you are still angry, and do not give the devil a foothold . . . Get rid of all bitterness, rage and anger, brawling and slander, along with every form of malice. Be kind and compassionate to one another, forgiving each other, just as in Christ God forgave you" (Ephesians 4:26–27; 31–32).

For my sake and the sake of my family, I *had* to work through this in a productive way. Unaddressed anger destroys. Vented wrongfully, it slashes those we love and bottled up it brews bitterness and self-destruction.

Bargaining

When situations feel out of control, a common response is to try to stabilize by reconstructing the past. Some plead with their spouses for reconciliation or propose changes to make the marriage work. Others secretly make deals with God, hoping to postpone the inevitable.

For me, this stage took the longest while I vacillated between pleading for a miraculous restoration and coming to terms with reality. I still wanted to believe the best about someone who demonstrated no signs of repentance or remorse. I constructed elaborate mental games, all with reconciliation as the prize. *If he comes to church on Sunday, then I know he wants me back, or if he's pleasant to me during the next child exchange, then I know he regrets what he did.* These strategies hung precariously on the unrealistic expectation that he would change his mind and heart.

Depression

It's important to dispel some common myths about depression. If behaviors and feelings differ from assumptions, people may erroneously conclude they aren't depressed.

My own struggles with depression came and went. Many times I thought I was making headway, only to have something happen and get knocked down again. Frustration perpetuated these cycles. I desperately wanted to do God's will but seemed to get nowhere. When I saw others in good and loving relationships their happiness felt unfair. This rollercoaster left me parched for hope and purpose. I was defeated and wanted to give up.

During one of those bouts, I wrote this:

My heart is sick—my heart is broken.
I am alone.
You turned your back when I cried for help.
Rejected and abandoned I long for relief,
Waiting to experience the breakthrough I was promised.
Waiting in great expectation and receiving nothing.
I wait . . . I wait . . . I wait.
I keep hoping . . . what's left to hope for?
My bottled-up anger exhausts me
Seeping out in disdain and despair.
Hope . . . is there any left for me?

We all cope differently. Sadness or downswings in mood are normal reactions to the magnitude of the pain in divorce. The challenge is seeing the fine line that exists between a normal grieving process and depression. The amount, severity, and length of symptoms determine whether someone has crossed the line into depression. When these symptoms become overwhelming and disabling, it's time to seek help.

Signs and symptoms of depression:

- Overwhelming guilt and feelings of helplessness, worthlessness, and/or hopelessness.

- Persistent feelings of sadness, anxiety, or numbness.

- Loss of interest or pleasure in hobbies, and activities.

- Appetite and/or weight changes.

- Sleep changes: oversleeping, insomnia, or early morning waking.

- Anger, irritability, or a short temper.

- Decreased energy, fatigue during even small tasks.

- Difficulty focusing and concentrating.

- Self-loathing. Strong feelings of worthlessness or guilt. Harsh self-criticism for perceived faults and mistakes.

- Self-medicating behavior: overeating, drugs, excessive use of alcohol, gambling, or shopping to cope with your feelings.

- Increase in physical complaints such as headaches, back pain, sore muscles, and stomach pain.

- Thoughts of death or suicide; suicide attempts.

There's a high correlation between suicidal feelings and divorce. During extreme depression people have difficulty seeing any hope. When this happens, it's critical to seek help and guidance to gain perspective. Satan, the enemy of our souls, isolates us, further perpetuating the lie that we don't matter. This is simply not true. Your life matters and you are important to the heart of God. He has a plan for you. Please get help and entrust your life and pain to him.

Acceptance

It took me three years to accept my marriage would never be restored. I circled through every stage of grief several times before I acknowledged the truth.

Coping with loss is deeply personal, a painful journey without a smooth path for easy travel. Because divorce is so common, many sense an expectation to grieve in a certain manner, or within a certain time frame. Grieving is part of healing, resisting it only prolongs the pain.

Fork in the Road

Divorce is a fork-in-the-road situation that forever changes us. The accompanying suffering brings us to critical life junctures. God never promises us a pain-free life, but instead warns us that in this life we *will* suffer.

The decision to hold on to our faith during uncertainty is challenging, but possible. At times, those who claim to love us will walk away, an almost unbearable experience. When this happens, we inch forward, remembering that in our deepest hurt, God is with us.

Sometimes we'll feel alone and unloved. I found that trying to live normally was excruciating. I couldn't bear the thought of others going on with their happy lives, when mine was so broken. I realize now, I didn't know what took place behind the closed doors of their homes any more than they could see behind mine. Perhaps those who seemed happy and secure were hiding their own pain.

When we finally come to God after exhausting ourselves trying to fix a situation, we often expect a swift resolution. New frustration sets in when our prayers aren't answered as quickly or in the way we think they should be. Doubt damages our trust and God's failure to answer on our schedule triggers a falling away for many. Feeling overlooked by God caused me to have a crisis of faith where I questioned his care and love for me.

I retreated inward, put on a mask, and pretended. People said, "You're so strong." But I wasn't. I was broken. Faking peace corroded my emotional compass. I needed to be transparent—with myself, with others, and most importantly, with God. He knew the weight of my grief. Even as I'd trusted his strength to sustain me, I needed to believe he'd carry my burdens. I read and reread his promises to me.

"Give your burdens to the Lord, and He will take care of you. He will not permit the godly to slip and fall" (Psalm 55:22 NLT).

> "Blessed be the God and Father of our Lord Jesus Christ, the Father of sympathy (pity and mercy) and the God [Who is the Source] of every comfort (consolation and encouragement), Who comforts (consoles and encourages) us in every trouble (calamity and affliction), so that we may also be able to comfort (console and encourage)

those who are in any kind of trouble *or* distress, with the comfort (consolation and encouragement) with which we ourselves are comforted (consoled and encouraged) by God. For just as Christ's [own] sufferings fall to our lot [as they overflow upon his disciples, and we share and experience them] abundantly, so through Christ comfort (consolation and encouragement) is also [shared and experienced] abundantly by us" (2 Corinthians 1:3–5 Amplified Bible).

Moment to moment I prayed for God to help me. At times I felt like I couldn't breathe. When overwhelmed by the ordinary tasks of my job and caring for my children, I cried out to him. He faithfully answered, carrying me minute-by-minute through each day.

He carried me then. He carries me now. And I have gained the confidence he will continue to do so. Healing always takes time, but through it all, I held on to God, keeping my thoughts directed toward him, and believing the promises in his Word.

"When you pass through the waters, I will be with you; and when you pass through the rivers, they will not sweep over you. When you walk through the fire, you will not be burned; the flames will not set you ablaze" (Isaiah 43:2).

"I have told you these things, so that in me you may have peace. In this world you will have trouble. But take heart! I have overcome the world" (John 16:33).

No matter how much we hurt, God's grace is greater, helping us overcome in any situation. Comfort doesn't guarantee he'll remove the problem or fix it right away. But he will guide us through, filling us with peace, molding our character, and drawing us closer to him.

Pain offers us a way to become more like Jesus, the one called "a man of sorrows and acquainted with grief" (Isaiah 53:3). He not only suffered the brutality of the cross, but he also felt the stab of rejection from his family and closest friends. Mocked throughout his ministry and scorned by the leaders who should have embraced him, he even suffered the withdrawal of his Father's presence at the end.

Jesus felt emotional, mental, spiritual, and physical pain because he is one hundred percent man and one hundred percent God. Because he was tortured and overcame, he knows and can relate to our suffering. Fully aware of the unjust agony he would endure, he willingly gave himself for us. He comforts us so that we can in turn offer comfort to others (2 Corinthians 1:4).

Safeguards

We all need safeguards due to our grief-impaired judgments that make us vulnerable. I erected safeguards to protect my heart and mind. Something as simple as a song on the radio could spark feelings that spiraled out of control, so I was careful about what I listened and viewed.

A long time passed before I could listen to lyrics where a man professed his undying love for a woman and not weep. Romantic dramas would initiate a two-to-three day mini-depression. Specific songs and movies made me ache over what I never had and always wanted. Each inflicted new injuries and aggravated old ones.

To counteract this, I surrounded myself with music that centered on the message of Christ's love. These songs elevated my outlook, a constant reminder that God was with me through every storm. I could bring him my brokenness again and again to receive the healing I desperately needed.

I also needed safeguards towards those felt at liberty to tell me what I should've done to avoid a divorce. Under the guise of helping, they stabbed me with criticism, causing more trauma. Their words gouged holes in my damaged sense of worth, rocking an already unsteady emotional equilibrium. After their initial shock and disbelief at my news, they repeated hurtful platitudes and useless advice.

So, I learned to make thoughtful choices about who I allowed to influence me. I surrounded myself with the truth of God's Word, separated myself from destructive verbal attacks, and made the decision to see myself through the eyes of Christ.

Love and support are critical in times of suffering. We need the company of other believers, to gain strength from their strength and to be encouraged by their confidence in God. Yet, sometimes the first people we choose when we're floundering in the stormy waters of trouble often criticize rather than offer a lifeline. Pat answers, glib quotations, and hasty advice rarely help.

Hurting people withdraw emotionally, if not also physically, to avoid these thoughtless attacks. Deprived of listening ears and accepting hugs, hurt causes a deeper pit of despair. How it must break the heart of God when his beloved is mistreated. When instead of being encircled with comfort, they're targeted with barbs of guilt and condemnation. This is where our focus must turn to Jesus.

Job

After Job's losses, recounted at length in the Old Testament, his three friends came and sat with him in silence. But in a brief time, they began to analyze him and offered days of unsolicited, accusing commentary. Their quiet presence and care turned critical when they listed everything he could've done differently to avoid his calamity.

At his lowest point, Job went from trusting God to questioning his care and sovereignty. Like us, during heartache and despair, Job didn't understand. His friends judged incorrectly. Their harsh attitudes alienated Job from them and from God, causing Job to be defensive. Instead of comforting him, they made his heartbreaking situation worse.

Then God stepped onto the scene. He proclaimed Job's true identity as his righteous son. No suffering, criticism, or human logic could take that away. Although Job was racked with pain, surrounded by critical friends, and unable to see an end to it, God still considered him one of the finest men to walk the earth. Job was finally freed from the label of desolation and despair, comprehending his identity as a child of the One True King.

Similarly, our suffering can't strip us of our identities as God's precious daughters. Desolation and grief may mar our beauty, steal our joy, and if we allow it, our very lives. The people we listen to affect how we see ourselves, and therefore helps or hinders our healing. If we adopt the disapproving view others thrust on us and accept their censure, we'll miss the Lord's perspective. This will stifle our hopes of healing, for only in the truth of God do we find our real identity. We must *never* forget who we are in Christ. And if we've never had a clear comprehension of our standing in Christ, now is the time to acquire it.

Reading the Bible consistently and praying frequently were keys to maintaining and cultivating my relationship with God. Often it was a moment-by-moment struggle. I read the Bible daily, sometimes several times. I prayed about everyday challenges as well as the disruptions in my life. At times, the only prayer I could utter was, "God get me through, give me the strength to face this moment." As the days turned into weeks and the weeks into months, I found myself getting stronger and stronger.

Staying connected to church helped keep me going. By remaining faithful in attendance, I had opportunities to serve. I worked in the children's ministry. I also met other young mothers going through similar struggles and was able to pray with them and offer support. Through this ongoing process, my life focus changed. When I deliberately concentrated on helping others, God renewed my sense of purpose, the catalyst for a much-needed breakthrough.

Proactive Approaches

Several consistent practices aided my journey to restoration—prayer, spending time in God's Word, professional counseling, introspection, exercise, as well as time with friends and family. Being in God's presence daily reminded me of his love and confirmed that I wasn't alone. In those precious moments with him, the Lord poured out comfort and peace. His presence gave my heart a much-needed father's embrace. I approached him without shame for my heavenly Father is always available for me and readily gives me his unconditional love.

At other times, God showed me areas of my life he longed to heal, broken places that were part of my dysfunctional *normal*. He also revealed parts of my character that needed cleansing and reshaping. Never stern, he gently brought all this to my attention.

Many believe God is a harsh taskmaster, demanding more than we can give and ready to strike us down. Knowing we can't meet his standard of perfection; we cringe and hide. When we do this, we align ourselves with our adversary and beat ourselves up, instead of bringing our brokenness to him.

When we try to fix things ourselves, we place ineffective patches on our lives. We fail when we compare God to our earthly parents. If we cling to the idea that we must be perfect before we can be accepted, we deny ourselves his restoration out of a misguided fear of judgment for our imperfection.

"For he has not despised or scorned the suffering of the afflicted one; he has not hidden his face from him but has listened to his cry for help" (Psalm 22:24).

God hears us and waits, for he is willing, but he won't force us. We must come to him, laying our burdens at the foot of the cross. Christ died, not only for our sins, but for our shame, weakness, and pain. He resolved it all on the cross at Calvary and is ready to bestow peace and wholeness.

Isaiah describes the great cost Jesus paid to restore our lives.

> "He was despised and rejected by mankind, a man of suffering, and familiar with pain. Like one from whom people hide their faces he was despised, and we held him in low esteem. Surely he took up our pain and bore our suffering, yet we considered him punished by God, stricken by him, and afflicted. But he was pierced for our

transgressions, he was crushed for our iniquities; the punishment that brought us peace was on him, and by his wounds we are healed. We all, like sheep, have gone astray, each of us has turned to our own way; and the Lord has laid on him the iniquity of us all" (Isaiah 53:3–6).

"See what great love the Father has lavished on us, that we should be called children of God! And that is what we are! The reason the world does not know us is that it did not know him" (I John 3:1).

"Let us then approach God's throne of grace with confidence, so that we may receive mercy and find grace to help us in our time of need" (Hebrews 4:16).

"Cast your cares on the Lord and he will sustain you; he will never let the righteous be shaken" (Psalm 55:22).

Healing Comes in Stages

In Mark 8:22–26 people brought a blind man to Jesus for healing, begging him to touch the man. In a unique response, Jesus took his hand, led him out of the village, and spit on his eyes. At first, the man saw men as trees walking. When Jesus put his hands back on the man's eyes, he saw clearly.

What a strange healing. Jesus could've simply spoken a word, but he didn't. The context of the story offers insights to this miracle. It follows the feeding of the four thousand, the opposition of the Pharisees who refused to see, and the dullness of the disciples to comprehend.

Christ demonstrated that he wasn't restricted to a single way of healing. Imagine the blind man's thoughts. He can't see and the person he trusted for healing spit on him.

Clarity came in stages, just as our healing comes a bit at a time—none of us sees our situation completely at the beginning. Partial sight, which raised his hopes, was followed by a second touch. Then, sharp vision resulted. Similarly, heart healing follows a progression, but when we do see, we discover we have an audience that will see what God has done for us.

Christ's instructions afterward seemed counterintuitive for the man whose newly acquired vision opened fresh possibilities for the future. Jesus told him not to return to the village where he'd been healed, but instead to go home. Seeing clearly changed everything. He was no longer a blind beggar dependent on others. He was now equipped to start a new way of life.

Many of us spend years blinded by the reality of our situation. Just like this man, God sees perfectly what we don't see and longs to give us sight. He wants to give us a new identity, a new beginning. Even when we feel alone, insecure, and can't stop our pain, we must remember that although he may not heal us right away, we can trust him through the process.

"O God, listen to my cry! Hear my prayer! From the ends of the earth, I cry to you for help when my heart is overwhelmed. Lead me to the towering rock of safety, for you are my safe refuge, a fortress where my enemies cannot reach me. Let me live forever in your sanctuary, safe beneath the shelter of your wings!" (Psalm 61:1–4 NLT).

Exchange despair for comfort in Christ.

TESTIMONY: SONIA,
DIVORCED AFTER FIVE YEARS OF MARRIAGE

After five years of a sad and difficult marriage, my husband left. The shock came one Saturday afternoon when I came home from an errand and realized he was gone. It was frightening. Without a job, I had no idea how I would support my children. A few days later God showed me that although my husband left, God was there.

I applied for a job several months before, but never heard from them. That very Monday, I got the call, was hired on the spot, and immediately went to work. By the time rent was due, I had enough money to pay it. Because I was in survival mode, it took several months before I could process the gravity of my situation. Then shock gave way to grief.

As a single mother of two, I needed to care for my children, while carrying the heavy burden of despair. My mornings were busy with mommy duties and at 2:00 pm I headed for my three-to-eleven work shift. My busy days contrasted the silent nights. I wept each night while I drove home, mourning the loss of my dreams. I never imagined I would be abandoned, divorced, raising my kids alone.

This "death" hurt, but I always stopped crying just before I made it home. This continued for two years until one day I heard a sweet voice saying, "Enough." I felt God talking to me and healing my heart. From then on, I never cried. As the sadness left, anger took over.

Anger gripped my life for several years. I retreated and focused only on me and mine. I didn't want to think about the possibility of loving again. I couldn't stand the thought of caring deeply for anyone. No potential relationship seemed worth it. Anger eventually shifted to emotional numbness.

Unable to give, I refused to receive as well. I erected walls around my heart that remained for many years. Now that time has passed, God has taken those barriers away and filled me with peace.

During my journey of increasing peace, I've leaned on God, and he has been faithful. I made new goals and discovered a restful quiet joy within, treasuring little moments and smiling at silly things. As I daily navigate the sea of life, I have a new point of view. I don't rush to reach some indefinable happy place down the road because I am happy right now.

I've gained some insights: God is awesome. He loves me. Pain doesn't last forever. Rushing leads to poor choices. The advice I respect and listen to will determine my future, so I choose wisely. Happiness is a choice and every moment in life is a gift.

I am grateful to God for my past and for the valuable lessons I've learned. I am also grateful for my present, for everyday is a new opportunity and an adventure. The lost girl has found herself. My beautiful babies are now wonderful teens that bring me joy. I've grown financially savvy, and money is no longer an issue. I returned to school and have a career I love. Best of all, I can dream again.

My Name Changer, God, has gently remolded my life. He has steadied me in daily practices like Bible reading and prayer that position me to hear him speak my true identity into my heart. Repetition of the truth erased the lies I believed, whether spoken to me by others or myself. The reality of my identity grew truer over time.

Christ gives us a new name:
COMFORTED.

CHAPTER TWO: GRIEVING THE LOSS

Prayer

Lord, I do not understand the circumstances surrounding me, sometimes I feel like I am drowning. I call on you because you alone are my lifeline. You are my strong tower, and I can take refuge in the shadow of your wings (Psalm 61:3; Psalm 91:4). Free me from negative emotions and help me to reach a place of wholeness in you. Jesus, you were pierced for my transgressions and crushed for my sin. Your punishment brought me peace and by your wounds I am healed (Isaiah 53:5). I call upon that healing for my soul. I lay down all depression, anxiety, anger, suicidal thoughts, and thoughts of revenge at the foot of the cross. Thank you, Lord, for the inner healing you are bringing to my life.

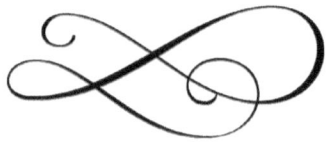

I waited patiently for the Lord; he turned to me and heard my cry.
He lifted me out of the slimy pit, out of the mud and mire;
he set my feet on a rock and gave me a firm place to stand.
He put a new song in my mouth, a hymn of praise to our God.
Many will see and fear the Lord and put their trust in him.

—Psalm 40:1–3

Reflection

Before answering these questions, ask the Holy Spirit to bring to mind the areas of your life addressed in this chapter which need healing and change.

1. Where are you in the stages of grief (denial, anger, bargaining, depression, acceptance)?

2. When do your wounded feelings make you feel trapped? What can you do to change this?

3. Who makes up your godly support network? If you don't have anyone, how can you find people to help you?

4.   Have you reached out to God and given him your pain? How have you asked him to help you with each step? If you haven't, what's stopping you?

5.   What in your life or influences do you need to evaluate and change?

THREE

Reconciliation Vs. Wishful Thinking

I t's difficult to reconcile our Christian faith with divorce. Pulpit messages proclaim hope, insisting God will heal even the most damaged marriages if the couple exercises enough faith. We hear countless testimonies of God's miraculous intervention for crumbling relationships. These words often produce guilt-laden thoughts when coupled with the wayward glances from those who "know" we didn't fight hard enough. Their looks imply our faith was too weak, that if it were stronger, we wouldn't be divorced.

I spent year after year praying for my husband's salvation. I wept, fasted, and pleaded, but my prayers went unanswered. After years of banging my head against a spiritual wall, I realized an inconvenient truth. No matter how hard we plead or pray, we can't force people to change. People choose how they live, even if it brings destruction to those around them. God never forces anyone to serve him.

Divorce is a Concession

I believe every marriage that can be saved should be saved. Even in cases of adultery or deceptive behavior, if there is true repentance from the offending spouse, then steps toward healing and reconciliation should take place. Forgiveness is always the higher law. Although God gives us a way out of a marriage following infidelity, his heart leans toward reconciliation. If both spouses work diligently with openness, humility, and repentance, a marriage will not only survive, but thrive.

I've seen many people walk away from their marriages because of an affair, only to regret it later. Despite genuine repentance on the part of the offending spouse, the betrayed spouse was either unable or unwilling to reconcile, believing the wound inflicted was too deep to overcome.

Repentance Vs. Remorse

There are different kinds of sorrow for sin. Some people have true sorrow and willingly work to repair broken love and trust. Others are only sorry they got caught. This divides people into two groups—possible reconciliation and wishful thinking.

A spouse who simply regrets getting caught will rationalize their behavior and justify their actions—clearly *not* repentant. It's a matter of the heart. Their actions and attitudes demonstrate an unwillingness to change, and they will inevitably fall back into similar patterns.

"For the kind of sorrow God wants us to experience leads us away from sin and results in salvation. There's no regret for that kind of sorrow. But worldly sorrow, which lacks repentance, results in spiritual death" (2 Corinthians 7:10 NLT).

Cognitive Dissonance
(When Actions Clash with Beliefs)

Many people feel sorry for the *effects* of their behavior and the pain they have caused, yet despite a show of remorse they see no reason to take the necessary steps for restoration. When people continually violate their own consciences, by engaging in adulterous relationships or committing habitual sins, they behave contrary to their morality or principles, resulting in cognitive dissonance.

When we act in opposition to our professed convictions and beliefs, we experience mental stress and discomfort—worldly remorse and worldly sorrow. A sense of sorrow alone doesn't guarantee humility before God or accepting responsibility for hurting others. Remorse without repentance blocks God's peace. Instead, the person continues down a bitter, self-destructive road.

I often thought I glimpsed signs my former spouse would repent. When I first confronted him, he appeared remorseful and shocked, yet relieved the truth was finally revealed. In one breath he apologized for his behavior and in the next justified them. During one period, he tried to change, a short-lived attempt motivated by all the wrong reasons. Instead of asking God to help him, he was only sorry I found out what he had been doing and continued to satisfy his unchecked cravings.

Even after the divorce was final, I watched for signs of willing change. I hoped he'd wake up and fight for his family. I forgave him and was willing to reconcile. My only condition was that he surrender his heart to Jesus and take steps toward repentance—the only way we could have a fresh start. For three years, I lived in this mind-torturing limbo.

Wishful Thinking

Wishful thinking believes something will come to pass, without evidence to validate that conviction. We cling to empty promises despite actions that negate them. Apologies are smoke screens, obscuring reality. I blindly clung to his words, desperate to believe he was sorry for destroying our family and that he did love me. I grew increasingly shattered and confused as he became an unrecognizable stranger.

It's difficult for us to understand a spouse's selfishness when we give our best to them. It's hard to realize their apologies were only voiced to placate us momentarily. It's incomprehensible to imagine they could be intimate with others, and care so little about us. When we have poured our love into another person's life, it's hard to accept these hurtful actions reflect the true state of their heart. Love is sacrificial. Selfishness only thinks of itself, taking no consideration of another.

Denial is powerful, hiding wounds in the beginning is like a cancer destroying us from the inside out. My desperate, flawed thinking blinded me to the malignancy of refusing to acknowledge the truth. Once the blinders were torn off, I had to face my situation. Denial was ravaging the future God had for me.

God Hates Divorce

The Word of God says he *hates* divorce. "For I hate divorce!" says the LORD, the God of Israel. "*To divorce your wife is to overwhelm her with cruelty*," says the LORD of heaven's armies. "So guard your heart; do not be unfaithful to your wife" (Malachi 2:16 NLT emphasis added).

I constantly asked, "Lord, if you hate divorce, why am I divorced?" Like many others, I focused on the first part of this passage, barely reading the rest, "to divorce your wife is to overwhelm her with cruelty."

When an object is whole, it can't be disassembled; in order to break, it must be shattered, torn, and dismembered. Divorce resembles an emotional trail of discarded, blood-covered fragments. God hates it because divorce demolishes victims, wounding the hearts of his beloved.

God knew how much my children and I suffered. He saw our tears and felt our pain, grieving with us over the demise of our family. He hated it. Through this process, I experienced his love in my worst moments and learned a magnificent truth. *God's love is greater than divorce.*

Destiny Suckers

Many of us stay and tolerate sins we should challenge, such as serial cheating, abuse, and addictions. We fail to take a stand and remain for a variety of reasons.

- We don't want to split up the family.
- We fear we're violating a biblical mandate.

- We don't value ourselves enough to know we are worthy of love.

- We're financially dependent on our spouse.

- We fear the unknown or the criticism of others.

A failure to immerse ourselves in God's Word leaves us susceptible to the condemnation of those who pressure us to stay in unhealthy situations. Many of us have relinquished the good life God designed for us by settling for a horrible present with the very person who is robbing us of that future.

These people are *destiny suckers*. They kill our potential, break our spirits, and make us believe the lie we don't deserve anything better. However, the problem isn't the destiny suckers, but us, when we allow ourselves to be their prey. Keeping the above reasons in mind, aware that our children may suffer, we must ask, "Lord, what do I do?"

Seeking God's Will

We must seek God's wisdom regarding how the Lord would have us think and respond (Proverbs 2). This means *we* must read the Bible, an excellent antidote for simply settling for the pronouncements others make about our life. We must approach God's words with confidence based on his promise to give us insight and understanding *if* we seek it.

This isn't a weekend only venture requiring a few hours. This is about the rest of our lives, our walk with God, the example we set for our children, and the command of the Lord to follow him fully. It will take time. We need to make notes and pray over what the Lord shows us. Using a spiral notebook or journal to record promises and insights is an excellent way to keep focused on what God says about us. Enlisting the prayers of trusted believers is also important for the search we are embarking on.

We must seek the answer like hidden treasure because it may not be readily available or easily seen. It may require difficult adjustments in viewpoint and behavior. It may require digging deep into the hidden recesses of our heart and mind. For some, staying in the marriage is the right answer. For others, a therapeutic separation can heal the broken parts of the relationship. Others may have to end the marriage. Therefore, maintaining a close relationship to God and his Word is vital in making the correct decision.

Theologians have a long history of debating the biblical guidelines for a believer to divorce. After studying the scriptures and other scholarly resources, I've come to understand two clear biblical justifications. The first is infidelity. "It has been said, 'Anyone who divorces his wife must give her a certificate of divorce.' But I tell you that anyone who divorces his wife, except for sexual immorality, makes her the victim of adultery, and anyone who marries a divorced woman commits adultery" (Matthew 5:31–32).

The second is abandonment by the unbelieving spouse.

"To the married I give this command (not I, but the Lord): A wife must not separate from her husband. But if she does, she must remain unmarried or else be reconciled to her husband. And a husband must not divorce his wife. To the rest I say this (I, not the Lord): If any brother has a wife who is not a believer and she is willing to live with him, he must not divorce her. And if a woman has a husband who is not a believer and he is willing to live with her, she must not divorce him. For the unbelieving husband has been sanctified through his wife, and the unbelieving wife has been sanctified through her believing husband. Otherwise your children would be unclean, but as it is, they are holy. But if the unbeliever leaves, let it be so. The brother or the sister is not bound in such circumstances; God has called us to live in peace. How do you know, wife, whether you will save your husband? Or, how do you know, husband, whether you will save your wife?" (1 Corinthians 7:10–16).

Many marriages between a believer and an unbeliever can continue. In fact, if this is the case, the Lord directs the believer to remain, not to look for "greener pastures." The believer should pray for her spouse and conduct herself in such a way as to lead her husband to the Lord.

However, when the non-believing spouse, or the spouse who once claimed to believe, but has left the faith, leaves, abandons his family, God allows divorce. He wants us to live in peace. The destruction from continuing the union would be worse than if it were dissolved. We have a higher law to uphold, God's law. This situation can be especially destructive to children in the home who learn maladaptive patterns and believe they are normal.

What About Abuse?

If there is violence, seek safety. I've counseled several women who were in severely abusive relationships who were advised to stay and "Work it out, because God hates divorce."

It's doubly tragic when abuse victims seek help and are given dangerous advice. At times, the facts about their situations are downplayed or not fully believed, causing more isolation and despair. Callous comments follow these suffering souls from those who think they understand, "Well if it's so bad, why doesn't she just leave?"

There are many dynamics surrounding abuse. Unfortunately, some in positions of leadership within the church are unaware of the underlying forces and provide poor guidance to victims.

God is for us, and he takes abuse seriously. If you find yourself in a physically or mentally destructive relationship, seek safe refuge. God hates divorce, but he also hates abuse. *More scriptures condemn abuse than address divorce.* Unfortunately, these are overlooked, leading to undue guilt and condemnation, perpetuating unhealthy and dangerous cycles.

We are special and beloved by God. Any form of abuse is unacceptable. Various Christian resources deal correctly with this subject. Seek those out as well as local domestic violence resources to attain help and safety.

Board of Directors

The decision to divorce was one of the most difficult choices I've ever made. I asked God repeatedly to help me and show me the right path. Additionally, I had a team of trusted men and women praying for me and my family. Lovingly named, My Board of Directors, I conferred with them when I had to make major decisions. "For lack of guidance a nation falls, but victory is won through many advisers" (Proverbs 11:14).

Emotional duress affected my feelings and skewed my perspective. My impulsive tendencies had brought profound consequences in the past, so I didn't want to act rashly, because now my family was on the line.

My Board of Directors were the only ones I fully trusted with my feelings and the details of my situation. I was transparent with them, knowing they had my best interests at heart. They knew my strengths and weaknesses and provided prayer, encouragement, advice, and at times, reproof. I accepted their correction, because it came from love, not criticism.

When I was in "the thick of it" and needed to make critical choices, I'd ask each one separately for advice and most of the time, their recommendations were the same. They helped me create boundaries and break my faulty codependent mindset.

Because I knew proceeding with divorce would have life altering implications, I consistently sought the Lord's guidance, wanting assurance that without a shadow of a doubt, I was doing the right thing. I included my "Board's" counsel. These careful, time-consuming steps let me say confidently that God delivered me from the relationship, which was destroying each member of my family. The time and energy I invested in trying to save it had blinded me to the dysfunction that consumed us all.

God alone tests the heart and knows a person's true intentions. There is purpose for each of our lives and we have a responsibility to be good stewards and not waste the talents and energy he has given us. We can squander much of our lives on fruitless things and make decisions that derail our destiny.

Through the fog of conflicting thoughts, I remained determined to put my hope on the unwavering truth of God's Word. I chose to believe his promises that he does have a good future and a hope for my children and me.

Exchange uncertainty for clarity in Christ.

TESTIMONY: GLORIA,
SEPARATED AFTER THIRTY-ONE YEARS OF MARRIAGE

After growing up in a Pentecostal home where my father was the pastor, I got married at the age of twenty-one. My husband was an army sergeant, and his parents were deacons in the church. I loved him deeply. He was my Prince Charming.

Young and naïve, the truth about him surfaced soon after our honeymoon. My first glimpse into his secret life came when I saw him stashing bottles of alcohol. This was the beginning of years of manipulation, adultery, along with physical and verbal assaults.

To the outside world, everything seemed fine. I hid the pain so well no one had an inkling of the abuse I endured. When I finally got the courage to admit it, I wasn't taken seriously. Several times I tried to get out, but the peer pressure and guilt from those who assumed to understand dragged me back into my cage.

Being a Christian in a troubled marriage was hard. I'd been taught that if things weren't right, it was my fault. I believed being a true Christian meant weathering the storm, praying more, fasting more, and being more submissive. Yet, no matter how hard I tried or how much I sought the Lord, things got worse.

I fooled myself into thinking God would miraculously change everything. He warned me many times to leave this sick relationship, but I couldn't understand how such a request would come from God. My faulty thinking almost cost my son's life and mine.

One day when my young adult son and I were out, my husband came home with a gun. While he was loading it, he told my daughter in a matter-of-fact way, "This bullet is for your mother and this one is for your brother." Because he harbored less animosity toward her, she was able to talk him into giving her the gun and then warn me. He planned our murders down to the last detail.

Many times we believe things we're told without seeking the truth from God's Word for ourselves. The Holy Spirit was prompting me to leave, but I didn't listen, because it didn't line up with my religious view of God. I thank God for his mercy, for without it I wouldn't be here today. I share my testimony hoping someone will learn from my mistakes.

Learning to discern the underlying motives of the offending spouse can open our eyes to the reality of repentance or remorse. What may masquerade as faith, can simply be wishful thinking about an outcome of reconciliation when no evidence supports those thoughts. A collection of trusted friends can offer the advice that will continue to untangle the threads of the scarlet letter of divorce and stitch words of wisdom on our soul that spell our true identity, our eternal names, in Christ.

Christ gives us a new name:
OVERCOMER.

CHAPTER THREE:
RECONCILIATION VS. WISHFUL THINKING

Prayer

Lord, I come before you today and I ask you to forgive me for the times I assumed to know what's best without coming to you first. I know you will work all things out for the good for those who trust you and are called according to your purpose (Romans 8:28). I ask for your help and strength in all my relationships. I ask that you help me discern the areas in my life and the lives of others I have not relinquished to you. I surrender _____ (name of person/s) to you. Give me discernment so I will not accept into my life anything that grieves you and is destructive to me.

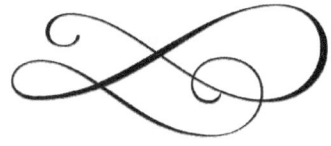

"As for me, I call to God, and the Lord saves me. Evening, morning and noon I cry out in distress, and he hears my voice. He rescues me unharmed from the battle waged against me, even though many oppose me. God, who is enthroned from of old, who does not change—he will hear them and humble them, because they have no fear of God. My companion attacks his friends; he violates his covenant. His talk is smooth as butter, yet war is in his heart; his words are more soothing than oil, yet they are drawn swords. Cast your cares on the Lord and he will sustain you he will never let the righteous be shaken."

—Psalm 55:16–22

Reflection

Before answering these questions, ask the Holy Spirit to bring to mind the areas of your life addressed in this chapter which need healing and change.

1. What circumstances and attitudes have led you and your spouse to divorce? Is your spouse repentant or remorseful? Is reconciliation possible?

2. Describe any situations where you need to take a stand and, if you haven't, what has stopped you?

3. Have you allowed yourself to be transparent with trusted, godly people? Why or why not?

FOUR

Letting Go of the Fantasy

ossing and turning in my bed, I imagined an all too familiar scene. I walk through the door and find an arrangement of brightly colored fresh flowers awaiting my arrival. Meanwhile phone messages proclaiming my greatness and expressions of remorse overload the inbox, "I was such a fool . . . how could I ever hurt you as I did?" Letters stacked high with ardent promises to fight for the marriage—whatever it takes. He approaches on bended knee pleading for forgiveness. Then reality slaps me in the face. These things never happened.

Instead, I was discarded. I couldn't understand this outcome after years of devotion and sacrifice; wasted effort grasping for a love that wasn't there.

To make matters worse, in his new life, my former spouse seemed happier than ever. He indulged in several vacations with his new girlfriend and wished that I would just get on with my life. I didn't matter. While I suffered, longing for a repaired relationship, he was completely over me.

Throughout our marriage, I spent so much time and energy fighting for the commitment I knew he could give and coping with the rest. I lived with chronic verbal and emotional abuse, hoping if he would finally realize how good I was to him, he'd come back.

For many of us, that day never comes. The fantasy our spouses will miraculously change and have a life-altering revelation continues to delay the healing process. I held on to that belief, confirmed countless times by others. Some were convinced my former husband would have a "Damascus Road Moment" and experience a dramatic conversion (Acts 9:1–19); a moment where God would speak to him in a supernatural way, and he would finally wake up and serve him. Their illusions nurtured false hope and made me doubt the truth I knew.

In hindsight, I realize that if I had *really* been perfect and performed every task to his expectations, it still wouldn't have changed the situation. He made the decision to put himself first and seek fulfillment outside of our marriage. I couldn't change that.

I needed to modify my inner focus and begin rebuilding my life. My futile pursuit of love and affirmation from him left me empty and broken. I had to face this reality with courage and let go of the fantasy of a miraculous reconciliation.

It's Not Supposed to be Like This

Divorce has been an especially difficult concept for me to grasp because it didn't fit into my Christian worldview. My prayers for reconciliation were godly. I wanted to do God's will and worked hard to avoid divorce. The longer my requests went unanswered, the more I questioned God's character and love for me.

The trajectory of my life was grossly different than the one I imagined. I felt overlooked, forgotten, and betrayed by God in my deepest time of need. I believed I knew his plan. Surely, he didn't want my marriage to end in divorce. I waited years for a miracle that never came.

Devastated, I'd become angry whenever I heard stories of God healing other marriages. I saw men cry at the church altar, reconciling their hearts to God. Their wives wept with joy for God's healing touch on their union. While I displayed a smile, in the depth of my heart, I grieved. This is what I always wanted, for my husband to love God so we could serve him together.

When a person fashions a desire based on God's Word and is assured that a certain outcome is in his plan, unanswered requests result in more questions than answers.

Sting of Rejection

The sting of rejection strikes in the most unexpected places. One incident occurred at a quinceañera, a defining moment in a young woman's life similar to a sweet sixteen party. In the Latin culture, this is a rite of passage where parents present their daughter to the world. At this ceremony, the young lady's father proclaimed a blessing upon her. His words were full of love and affirmation, letting not only his daughter, but everyone present know how much he valued and esteemed her. It was magical.

I cried through it all, not tears of joy, but of sorrow. I thought about how different my life might have been if my father had affirmed me. In his eyes, instead of lovely, I was a nuisance. Instead of beautiful, I was fat. To this day, the little girl inside me wishes my father would have seen me as lovely. This desire caused me to seek acceptance and love in the arms of my husband. He too echoed the same message. Instead of lovely, I was a nuisance. Instead of wanted, I was a waste. My efforts at being a good wife were never enough. I worked, maintained our home, cooked our meals, and tried to be a good mother, but I didn't measure up. I carried a deep insecurity and was afraid of failing or being vulnerable around him.

Constantly hearing devaluing messages from those who are supposed to love and protect cut to the core. God knew how I felt even before I put those feelings into words. He knew the anguish and doubt in my heart.

I've cried out many times to my heavenly Father, seeking his embrace. I asked him to replace the messages meant to destroy me with his message that restores; to bind up my wounds and dry my tears. Honesty in these feelings led the way for God to begin the healing process in my heart. In the challenging times I felt his embrace and heard him whisper, "Yes, you are enough . . . I am proud of you . . . You make me smile."

Knowing God loves me isn't enough, I must believe it. I continually draw on him for strength and seek him to discern truth from lies. I choose to believe who he says I am and reject the lie I don't matter or that I'm not good enough.

In times of confusion and doubts he provides much needed reassurance and comfort. God is not like my former spouse. He never turns his back on me. Instead, he holds me close and helps me understand that my value does not come from my father, a husband, or any other person. My value comes from him. He says I'm precious. He highly esteems and values me, so much that he sacrificed his best for me.

The Beauty of God's Love

God shows me his constant love at random times throughout the course of my day. Sometimes during my morning quiet time, I read a devotional that addresses the exact things I'm thinking about; or my children perform an act of kindness that speaks love to me. Other times in conversation, a comment coincides with a particular prayer request or voices encouragement.

God cares about the details of our life (Psalm 37:23). If we take the time to notice, we will see his presence all around us. His love and peace are greater than we can imagine. If I had continued to exhaust myself trying to gain that type of love from another person, I would have been blind to all of God's loving details in my life. "Neither height nor depth, nor anything else in all creation, will be able to separate us from the love of God that is in Christ Jesus our Lord" (Romans 8:39).

His Word says I'm the apple of his eye (Zechariah 2:8). He stitched me together in my mother's womb and knows me from the inside out. I am valuable to him (Psalm 139:13–14). He loves me completely and uncon-ditionally, with an everlasting love that doesn't change in spite of my imperfections (Ephesians 3:17–18). He thinks of me and is with me always (Psalm 139:17–18:17). His love makes me brave and with him nothing is impossible (I John 4:18; Mark 10:27).

The destruction of my life provided the environment where I attained a deeper understanding of God's love. Through the brokenness I have not only known, but have also felt, his love in a palpable way. I have been forced to draw closer to God because he has been my only lifeline.

No Easy Answers

I don't know why God saves some marriages and not others. I don't understand why he intervenes in some situations and not in others. Perhaps John the Baptist felt the same way when, after years of serving God, he ended up in a dungeon and was beheaded.

While in the dungeon, deep in despair, John had a crisis of faith (Matthew 11:1–19). He questioned what he knew to be true—was Christ really the Messiah? John dedicated his life pointing others to Christ and God the Father spoke audibly to John at Jesus' baptism. However, in the bottom of the dungeon with no reprieve in sight, his emotions temporarily blinded his heart from the truth. He questioned because he didn't understand the terrible turn of events in his life. He couldn't understand why Christ was allowing him to languish in a dungeon when John knew Jesus had the power to save him.

John's amazing faith was rooted in the miraculous deliverance of the Israelites from slavery in Egypt. Knowing God's power, he possibly wondered why God hadn't intervened on his behalf. I can only speculate the questions filling his mind: *"Why hasn't Jesus intervened?" "Jesus, where are you? Don't you care about me?"*

John's disciples presented his concerns to Jesus. Just like John we can bring our pain and doubt to him. Christ didn't belittle John or his faith. On the contrary, Jesus spoke well of him and reminded us of his godly example. Jesus reassured John, just like he reassures us. He is the Messiah. He has a greater plan than we can imagine.

In the end, John never got a miraculous release from his prison cell. With so much emphasis placed on how God can alleviate our trials, many have been conditioned to think we should be exempt from suffering. But as John's life demonstrates, that isn't the case.

God never promised days without sorrow. He did promise our anguish will end on the other side of eternity in Heaven. While on earth we will suffer, be persecuted, rejected, and endure cruel treatment. Deliverance from affliction doesn't validate our godliness. *It's what we do in the midst of suffering that defines our character.*

When we don't understand the circumstances of our lives we'll question whether God is really listening. Why? Is the prevailing question. In those times be honest. Talk to God; tell him your pain and ask him your questions. Seek him in prayer. Be willing to wait for an answer. Accept a season when he seems silent. Continue in faith and patience. Nothing catches God by surprise. During tragic circumstances, when we pull our hearts back to God, our perspective changes from why to whom.

John spoke truth in a time and place where darkness reigned. He never gave up, never surrendered, and never compromised. He stood out, and for that he suffered. His reward for refusing to compromise God's Word was death.

John's life and impact stretched far beyond anything he could have conceived. His life and death remain for us as a vivid portrait of the struggles of our faith and how we can come to God with our questions and doubts. It is a stark reminder of how we lift our view from the here and now to the perspective of eternity.

His legacy continues.

Exchange why with whom.

TESTIMONY: LAURA PETHERBRIDGE,
AUTHOR OF *WHEN "I DO" BECOMES "I DON'T"*

I was a new Christian when my husband left. Only two years after our "I do," he decided "I don't." Discovering he was already in a new relationship crushed me.

After my parents divorced when I was eight, I focused on one goal, "I will never be divorced." My husband's choice to switch beds not only made the tears flow, but also shook my faith to the core. God clearly hated divorce and I did too. So why did he allow it to happen? I wanted the Lord to wake my husband up to his poor choices. I longed for a glorious, reconciled marriage like those I'd read about in Christian books.

All the while, I wondered if it was my fault. I questioned whether God was mad at me. Because I believed God answered every prayer, I couldn't understand why he failed to answer mine. I felt abandoned as my fervent requests seemed to be ignored.

Much time passed before I realized that even though I cried, prayed, and begged God to restore my marriage, He wasn't going to handcuff my husband to my refrigerator. Although leaving was my spouse's choice, I had to deal with the aftermath.

Emotional and spiritual devastation blocked my efforts to pray. Pleading before God took place as I stretched out on the floor, listening to Christian music on my stereo (it was 1984). Too emotionally exhausted to put my wounds into words, I relied on the lyrics to shape my cries to God. I later learned that many of the songs were words of scripture and understood why they helped so much.

While fighting persistent thoughts of suicide, music provided a way to cry out to God when I could find no words. In this dark period, music supported my days which stretched between life and death.

Thankfully, my loving church family stood beside me. They encouraged me, prayed for me, invited me, and loved on me during those grueling months of darkness, sin, and loss.

Jesus never let me go. Even though I sporadically turned from him, and tried to ease the pain with human foolishness, he never gave up on me. Instead, he wooed me back into his arms. He let me know in numerous ways that I was his beloved, and that his love would never fail or abandon me.

Divorce strengthened my faith, leading me to understand that Jesus alone provided my worth and identity. In addition, it taught me that marriage didn't complete me—only Christ completes me.

More than thirty-two years later, I still remember that divorce season, but now my scars serve a higher calling.

Broken marriages often leave fantasy stories of restoration behind, nurtured by those who are wounded by well-intentioned friends. A Christian worldview aims our hearts toward permanency, not dissolution. When trying to discern the truth of who we are in the ruins of divorce, we often hear the early voice of a demeaning parent that led us unwittingly to a spouse who continued the verbal destruction. But God has better plans, with a foundation in the perfect life and sacrificial death of the Lord Jesus. Our embedded wrong identity can be changed by the one who knows our true name from all eternity. And, so, we continue to release the pain and receive the healing.

Christ gives us a new name:
HEALED.

CHAPTER FOUR: LETTING GO OF THE FANTASY

Prayer

Lord, help me to remember that your ways are higher than my ways; your thoughts higher than my thoughts (Isaiah 55:8–9). Keep my focus on you even when things are not going the way I hoped. I pray you would help me let go of my past and the words and actions taken against me. Deliver me from any hold the past has on my mind and emotions. Purify my heart and emotions and restore to me all that has been lost. When I am drowning in a sea of pain and hopelessness, lift me up Lord Jesus. Like Peter, keep me from drowning as I keep my eyes on you (Matthew 14:22–33).

"The righteous cry out, and the Lord hears them; he delivers them from all their troubles. The Lord is close to the brokenhearted and saves those who are crushed in spirit. The righteous person may have many troubles, but the Lord delivers him from them all; he protects all his bones, not one of them will be broken."

—Psalm 34:17–20

Reflection

Before answering these questions, ask the Holy Spirit to bring to mind the areas of your life addressed in this chapter which need healing and change.

1. Are you struggling with fantasies of reconciliation when all evidence points to the contrary?

2. Do you feel let down by God? In what ways?

3. Have unanswered prayers caused you to doubt God's love and his willingness to help you?

4. Take some time to fully examine your thoughts and emotions, then write down the areas where you feel let down. Pray over each area and talk to God about your pain and questions.

FIVE

I Will Try to Fix You

*N*o one understands him the way I do. If I love him hard enough, he'll change. Perhaps if I pray more, am more fun, or lose weight, he'll be happy. I know my love will help him through. Sounds romantic and loyal, to love someone with such intensity that you'd sacrifice everything to try to make them happy.

It's a lie.

Constantly working to earn love and admiration causes us to compromise our integrity, creating the vicious cycle of codependency.

Codependency

Codependency is a need to control and rescue people by fixing their problems in a never-ending quest to gain their love and acceptance. Instinctively, the one who becomes a rescuer believes his or her love will help the other person mature and grow. Over time the rescuer becomes an enabler, facilitating dysfunctional and maladaptive patterns, and thus, the pattern of codependency evolves.

As a strong-willed person capable of confronting situations when they arise, I viewed the word codependent as a label for weakness. I considered my efforts to help my husband as proof of loyalty. Pride and shame kept me from revealing the difficulties in the marriage. I was blind to the truth—*I was an enabler in a codependent relationship.*

I spent incredible amounts of time and energy doing things to help my husband get what he wanted, believing that if I made him happy, he would love me. I thought if he could achieve his professional goals or reach a particular place of success in his studies, he would be content and appreciate the family he had. Sadly, my efforts failed. Instead, he criticized me and my efforts endlessly. He was never satisfied.

This is emotional abuse.

Proverbs 15:4 says, "A gentle tongue is a tree of life but a perverse tongue crushes the spirit."

My spirit was crushed.

My epiphany came one night when I was eight months pregnant with our son. After one of our numerous fights, I reached an end. At 3:00 a.m. I got in my car and drove away, not knowing where to go or what to do. I stopped at the local coffee shop and cried for about half an hour in the parking lot before calling my sister, who rushed to my side. My world was chaotic and uncontrollable, and I couldn't understand why. After talking for quite some time, she said, "Cary, you're in an emotionally abusive relationship."

At first the words just bounced around in my head. Emotionally. Abusive. Relationship. Then the light bulb went on. "Yes! You're right." I stared at her. "Why didn't you ever tell me?"

I had *no* idea.

If we are only at peace when the other person is satisfied, we're in a codependent relationship. When we reach a place where our happiness is dictated by another person's actions, reactions, and responses, we are hurting ourselves.

Experiencing the world around us with this faulty mindset, makes it difficult to understand what "normal" looks like. I grew up in a home riddled with dysfunction and codependence. I married and repeated the same patterns, unaware my relationship was emotionally abusive, until I was confronted with the ugly truth.

My sister's clear statement forced me to change the perception of my life. I studied to gain insight into my own faulty patterns and how I had allowed them to evolve. I was furious at myself for not recognizing them sooner, for digging my head in the ground waiting for a magical change to my situation. Fear of confrontation and my skewed projections, along with wanting to believe the best in him further eroded my sense of worth and brought destruction to my life.

Emotional abuse is overlooked because there are no visible wounds. Many women in codependent relationships with emotionally abusive husbands don't understand or see the cycle in their lives. I feel great compassion for men and women who are on this never-ending quest for love, value, and respect from a spouse. Unfortunately, the one they seek love and validation from, the very person whose opinion matters the most, is the one inflicting the greatest damage.

I have worked with women who have given twenty, thirty, even fifty plus years to a man who never valued them. Their partners demanded love, loyalty, and service, while never giving back a bit of compassion. Their emotional state saddens me because, I lived it. Like many others, I wept over the rejection, my inability to answer my children's questions, and my feelings of hopelessness and helplessness.

As a clinical social worker, I've seen both sides of the spectrum. I've seen men care for their beloved through major medical ailments such as cancer, Alzheimer's, and other diseases. I've also seen emotionally battered women love and care for their husbands through various health trials but be abandoned in their time of need or medical crisis.

My fondest memories in the field have been of men who lovingly retold stories of their dance partner for life who were now plagued with dementia. These men cared for their wives with love and patience. I recall one particularly moving story of love and compassion while I was still married, I drove home in tears realizing my relationship bore no similarities. Instinctively, I knew I would've been abandoned at the first sign of a serious health problem.

Denial dominates codependent relationships. Instead of a mutual effort to get to the root cause of ongoing conflicts and dysfunction, the enabler is blamed. We accept that guilt, believing that if we were better wives or husbands, or better Christians who prayed and fasted more, then positive change would come. Understanding my role in the dysfunction broke through the cloud of denial and prompted me to discover what God had to say in the Bible.

Love, joy, and peace aren't just feelings. They're a way of life. The only way to have these as constant companions is through maintaining a right standing with God by seeking his will.

God didn't create us to be doormats. He established marriage as a covenant where both partners are charged to love and cherish each other. When we care God's way, we think of the other person first. In contrast, selfish partners rarely think of anyone but themselves, and by manipulating their codependent spouses' need for approval, they engrain a cycle where they are constantly catered to.

Boundaries

God gives us free will—the right to choose. Yet some of us mistakenly think we can make and enforce decisions on and for others. We impose our will by trying to convince them we have the best solutions for their problems. Our well-intended advice falls on deaf ears, frustrating us all. Whether we are interacting with an abusive spouse, a rebellious child, a difficult parent, a ruthless coworker, or some other difficult person, we cannot take responsibility for another person's actions for they too, have free will. However, we can determine *our* responses and not carry the burden for another's poor choice. Ultimately, we decide how others will either *infect* or *affect* our lives.

Boundaries are critical. When my former husband continued his self-serving lifestyle, I could no longer allow his choices to dictate my happiness and my future. It wasn't good for either of us for me to continue enabling, and at times, mothering him. He needed to face the consequences of his decisions, and I had to allow it. My constant interference blocked the exercise and consequences of his free will.

There are Biblical guidelines for setting boundaries designed to bring reconciliation and peace.

> "If another believer sins against you, go privately and point out the offense. If the other person listens and confesses it, you have won that person back. But if you are unsuccessful, take one or two others with you and go back again, so that everything you say may be confirmed by two or three witnesses. If the person still refuses to listen, take your case to the church. Then if he or she won't accept the church's decision, treat that person as a pagan or a corrupt tax collector. "I tell you the truth, whatever you forbid on earth will be forbidden in heaven, and whatever you permit on earth will be permitted in heaven. "I also tell you this: If two of you agree here on earth concerning anything you ask, my Father in heaven will do it for you. For where two or three gather together as my followers, I am there among them" (Matthew 18:15–20 NLT).

First, when someone wrongs us, instead of confronting the situation we may want to ignore it, gossip, or become resentful. However, we are instructed to go to the person and talk with them one-on-one and forgive as often as needed. This enables restoration.

Second, if the first step fails, a private discussion including two or three neutral third parties should take place. These individuals serve as mediators in the dispute and help clear any miscommunication or misconceptions. This conversation isn't meant to be vindictive or judgmental. Instead, it's meant to bring resolution to the conflict.

Finally, if the offending person doesn't express repentance for their actions and willingly decides to continue in destructive behaviors, a boundary must be put in place. The enabler is the one who must make *this* decision because abusers are happy with the status quo.

Although, we need to continue to pray for that person, we must separate ourselves from the consequences of their decisions. This means not taking responsibility for their behavior or fixing the problems their actions cause. Although every situation is different, here's an example. If your spouse is chronically late to work because of excessive drinking, don't call his employer and offer an excuse for his tardiness. Let him face the full consequence of his behavior, even if it includes termination.

In the verses before and after this passage, Jesus makes it clear that he doesn't want any of his sheep to perish, even the wayward ones. However, when we fail to implement boundaries and continue to act as rescuers, we inhibit God's work in the life of a person. When we are intent on saving someone from the consequences of their actions, we get in the way. We need to acknowledge that a rock bottom experience may be the only way for that individual to look up to the One who can truly rescue.

Our job is to speak the truth in love, forgive, pray for him or her, and stop our enabling behavior. We can't change people, only God can. Our words will fall on deaf ears if the spouse chooses to continue in a destructive path of temporary pleasure and indulgence. So we need to say less to them and pray more about the issues that bother us.

Setting boundaries in a toxic relationship is difficult. Boundaries are clear expectations and limits for yourself and others. They begin with a careful evaluation of the situations in our lives. By looking inward, we start to identify how we have contributed to maladaptive patterns that are expressed outwardly. Perhaps we have made excuses for unhealthy habits. We may have acted in "helpful" ways, hoping our actions would lead to change. Or we have shut down our emotional responses, ignored situations, or reacted in passive aggressive ways.

Actions speak louder than words. I recommend saying nothing when someone infringes on boundaries you have clearly established. Instead, take action. To handle emotional abuse, you might simply say, "I'd like to discuss this issue with you, but I won't be spoken to this way. When you're able to speak kindly, we can try again." Then walk away. Do not engage. Honor the clear parameters of acceptable behavior you set.

Those in your life will accept, resist, or ignore your new stand. Once you have stated specific limits, you *must* maintain them enlisting all your strength of character. If you don't follow through, the boundary is useless.

Emotional manipulation succeeds because we allow it. Once we identify the situations where we have succumbed to manipulation, we must speak our truth. Then we must live by that truth, stand our ground, and refuse to be dominated.

We can't continue to enable other's destructive behavior patterns without, at the same time, inflicting damage on ourselves and the children in our family. We must seek God's wisdom, put boundaries in place, and by faith trust God to help us move forward in a direction that pleases him.

Peacemaker vs. Peacekeeper

"Blessed are the peacemakers, for they will be called children of God" (Matthew 5:9).

Jesus came to this world as a peacemaker. Does this mean he was a doormat for all humanity? Absolutely not! He treated everyone with love and respect, suffering with those who suffered and providing healing and restoration to many. He was uncompromising and spoke the truth with authority against those who misused God's Word for personal agendas. While he was gentle, he was also assertive and confronted when necessary. He never gossiped or complained. His "yes" was "yes" and his "no" was "no."

In Matthew 21, when Christ overturned the tables at the temple, it was out of righteous indignation at the misuse of his Father's house, not to show off his power. When he was treated unfairly, mocked, betrayed, and looked down upon, he never used his power to protect or exalt himself. He did not allow the opinions of others to affect his self-worth or stop him from what he needed to do. Completely focused on his assignment, instead of looking for affirmation from others, he turned his attention to his heavenly Father.

We can apply this outlook to our own lives. Instead of allowing the opinions of others to dictate who we are, we must remember *whose* we are. Our identity and self-worth do not come from others, but from God. Our heavenly Father tells us we are precious and beloved, revealing in his Word that each of us has been created uniquely and in his image. Since Jesus knew this, the mockery of others couldn't shake this clear and accurate view of himself. Nor could it deter him from his mission. Most of the time, he ignored the naysayers. When he did confront them, his bold truth counteracted their lies.

Peace*keepers,* on the other hand, avoid confrontation. Silenced by fear, they don't speak up when they should. They may want to, but self-preservation and the need to avoid conflict often win. Peacekeepers harbor resentment because they are often taken for granted and feel used.

To avoid conflict, peacekeepers may use passive aggressive strategies to mask their feelings. This is confusing because it's hard to know which stances are genuine. Some common ploys are sarcasm, the silent treatment, verbal criticism, deliberately not doing something that is asked or purposely doing something to offend and withholding intimacy and praise.

On the contrary, a peace*maker* confronts the truth in love despite the discomfort it may cause. Peacemakers want justice to prevail and don't back down from opposition. They love others and seek what is best for those around them. Even when they're at fault, instead of responding out of self-preservation, they admit their mistakes, apologize, and make every effort to reestablish peace in the situation. Peacemakers are uncompromising in truth, putting the interests of others above their own.

Before confronting others, we must evaluate our motives. Peacemakers will shape their comments in light of the following questions.

- Why am I confronting?
- Am I defensive or objective?
- Is it better to ignore the situation?

"And we urge you, brothers and sisters, warn those who are idle and disruptive, encourage the disheartened, help the weak, be patient with everyone. Make sure that nobody pays back wrong for wrong, but always strive to do what is good for each other and for everyone else" (1 Thessalonians 5:14–16).

Being a peacemaker is difficult. Instead of enjoying the instant gratification of giving people a piece of our mind or putting them in their place, we must practice the discipline of self-restraint. So, we must control our emotions. Prayerful reflection and a plan to underreact based on past experiences will enable us to identify the situations that unleash negative emotions. As a result, we can cool heated emotions with our responses.

Heart of Saul vs. Heart of David

I Samuel 15 records why God rejected Israel's first king, Saul. When he was sworn into office, Saul felt unworthy and tried to hide. Although he felt insignificant, God granted him a great honor.

As time passed, Saul became increasingly proud, self-sufficient, and arrogant. After he willingly disobeyed a direct command from the Lord he rationalized and justified his disobedient behavior. Despite a rebuke from the prophet Samuel who told him the kingdom would be torn from his hands, Saul cared more about the opinion of the people. He never took responsibility for or repented of his actions. Instead, he pleaded with the prophet to accompany him so the people would not lose faith in him (I Samuel 13).

Early in his life Saul had a genuine relationship with the Lord. He sang and even prophesied in his name. Initially, Saul wanted to be a good king, but the power went to his head. He refused to humble himself and accept correction, a pattern which prevailed the rest of his life.

After Saul willfully severed his relationship with God, he deteriorated physically, mentally, and emotionally. He had no peace and experienced hallucinations, jealousy, delusions of conspiracy, lack of sleep, and rage. The descriptions of his extreme emotional and mental instability can be equated in today's medical terms with schizophrenia paranoid type. Instead of flourishing under God's direction, he self-destructed under the weight of his pride and disobedience.

In contrast, David is described in the Bible as "a man after God's own heart" (1 Samuel 13:14; Acts 13:22). While tending sheep as a young man, David passed the time by playing his lyre and singing songs of praise to God. He maintained this attitude of worship as a young adult when he faced the wrath and persecution of Saul.

After various trials, David became the king of Israel, but peace in the kingdom made him complacent. His heart and mind wandered leading him down a trail of adultery and murder. Despite these atrocities, God called him a man after his own heart. How can this be?

Unlike Saul, when David was confronted with his sin, he repented. He recognized his errors and came humbly before the Lord. David wasn't perfect, yet he exemplified the kind of humility God seeks. We all fail. However, our reactions when we're confronted by our failures demonstrate our commitment or lack of it toward God.

We need to identify the habits of those in our lives. If they repeat the same destructive patterns and behaviors time and time again with no intention of changing, we must resist. We cannot allow those who have a heart like Saul to control our lives. We need to stop being manipulated and act according to Christ's truth.

Exchange manipulation with truth.

TESTIMONY: PHYLLIS,
DIVORCED AFTER TEN YEARS OF MARRIAGE

I find it hard to revisit my endless race of trying to change my husband. I pray my truth gives you courage to turn that corner and stop running the same race I did.

Changing my husband wasn't always something I tried to do. I didn't have a clear understanding of the toxic nature of our relationship. For years I told myself we were fine. Then one morning everything came crashing down. My worst nightmare became a reality . . . infidelity!

I learned this awful truth while getting our children ready for the day. My heart was shattered. I gasped for air. My mind went a million different directions. In those moments, I decided to fight for my marriage which meant changing him. In order to change him, I had to change myself.

I prayed harder (because if I prayed harder, God would bring him home). I also began dieting and lost an unhealthy amount of weight in a short amount of time. I wanted to get his attention away from the other woman.

I was disgusted with myself and hated my body after three children. Perhaps if I looked better, he would want me again. I cooked meals the nights he came home because the way to a man's heart is through his stomach, right? I removed all boundaries in the bedroom. He would be gone for days at a time. But if passionate sex was what he wanted, I made sure that's what I gave him. I deluded myself into thinking that if I continued this way, I would win his heart again.

After a few years of this vicious cycle, I experienced my defining moment. While home with my children, I received the devastating news that he had started a second affair with another woman.

This time I reacted differently. Rage I'd never felt rose up. I screamed hateful profanity and threw things. I punched my fist through the wall more than once. After what seemed like hours, I stopped, physically exhausted. I was soaked with sweat and tears. My fists were bloody. I could no longer stand and collapsed to the floor. Tears fell. I kept shaking.

Then a soft voice said, "Mama, are you okay?" My little girl had watched my whole explosion from the corner of my room.

I realized that in my efforts to change my husband, I lost myself. I made him my priority and dragged my children with me. I had to learn to let go of my old image of what a godly wife was. God doesn't call us to accept that kind of treatment, and to do it in his name. Yes, we are to forgive these hurtful offenses. However, forgiveness does not imply what they did was okay. Allowing God to heal your heart and seeing yourself the way he sees you is key.

When I finally understood the change that had to take place was not in him but in me, everything turned around. I placed boundaries. He was no longer able to come and go from my home as he pleased. He had to abide by a schedule. I withdrew intimacy and only communicated about the children. I stopped personal communication and ended conversations about us getting back *together. I went to court and filed for child support, which began the process for divorce proceedings.*

These changes were difficult, and he fought me every step of the way. Yet, each one empowered me. I finally began to feel like myself again, not an object desperately trying to win the love of a person who didn't want me. The journey has been long, but with time and lots of God's mercy and grace, I have experienced healing.

The journey to living out the name God bestows requires his love showing up through friends, family, and in encouraging words read and heard. The changes he makes include working through our genuine repentance and becoming strong, loving peacemakers, not flailing peacekeepers. Being wakened to his truth and making healthier emotional choices gives God all the glory.

Christ gives us a new name:
PEACEMAKER.

CHAPTER FIVE: I WILL TRY TO FIX YOU

Prayer

Lord, I recognize there are areas and people in my life I have not fully surrendered to you. Align my thoughts to your thoughts so the mind of Christ can be fully manifested in me (I Corinthians 2:16). I ask that you help me see and understand the maladaptive patterns in my life and give me the strength and the strategies to deal with them in a way that honors you. Help me to confront when necessary and to establish peace in every area of my life (Romans 12:18). I can only do this in your strength, so I ask you now Holy Spirit to equip me for the task at hand (Hebrews 13:21).

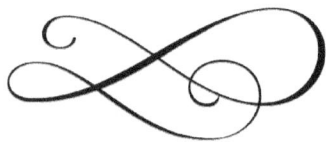

"I will listen to what God the Lord says; he promises peace to his people, his faithful servants—but let them not turn to folly. Surely his salvation is near those who fear him, that his glory may dwell in our land. Love and faithfulness meet together; righteousness and peace kiss each other. Faithfulness springs forth from the earth, and righteousness looks down from heaven."

—Psalm 85:8–1

Reflection

Before answering these questions, ask the Holy Spirit to bring to mind the areas of your life addressed in this chapter which need healing and change.

1. Are you in a situation where you're trying to "fix" someone? Do you find yourself in a parenting role with your spouse? List specific things you are doing that need to change immediately.

2. What destructive patterns exist in your relationship? What factors make it clear you need to take a stand? What boundaries need to be implemented?

3. How will you respond to violated or ignored boundaries?

4. List the areas in your life where you have been a peacekeeper instead of a peacemaker. Make a step-by-step plan for change.

5. Think of situations that try your patience. How will you stay calm and resist the urge to get even or avoid the peacekeeper pitfalls?

SIX

Temptation

eparation and divorce result in crushing loneliness. Constant reminders of your "singleness" are everywhere, from love songs on the radio to those awkward social gatherings echoing you are a party of one. Everyone around you is either getting engaged or is happily married. When you're with family and friends you feel like a third wheel or worse, a no wheel, alone on a Friday night.

You go home to an empty house day after day, and sleep in an empty bed night after night. Sure, you have friends, but it's not the same. When the lights go out, the silence is deafening.

Then, when you're most vulnerable, a man from your past or present rears his handsome head saying words your broken heart longs to hear. He'll stroke your ego telling you how beautiful and wonderful you are. You'll constantly think about him, hope to run into him, and dream about secret encounters. His attentions soothe your anguished heart, erasing pain and despair. You'll wake up with him in your thoughts, energized by exhilarating feelings you thought had died, like a schoolgirl with a crush.

Beware. This trap is from the enemy of your soul.

It took time for me to understand how deeply rejection and betrayal affected me. As a woman, I felt devalued and considered being intimate with a man to soothe my wounds and momentarily stroke my ego. The idea that someone would desire me provided much-needed assurance. While my pain could have been temporarily satiated, the fleeting pleasure would've left a gaping hole in my heart. Used and once again abandoned, I would have continued the cycle.

My children provided a safeguard because caring for them meant expectations and responsibilities. The difficulty came, especially in the beginning of our separation, when they went with their father. Coming back to an empty house left me alone with my thoughts, magnifying the ache. The silence and loneliness overwhelmed me.

Matthew 26:41 clarifies the challenge of temptation—the spirit is willing, but the body is weak. The strongest temptations come when we want something and are vulnerable. Our desire to be cared for and admired, is normal, especially when our hearts have been torn into a million pieces. We want companionship and long to be loved.

Temptation isn't a sin but giving in is. Feelings are deceptive and can cause us to rationalize and surrender to temptation. These justifications have a sneaky way of leading us down a path of self-destruction. Yet through it all, *our feelings don't determine our godliness; our actions do.*

"The heart is deceitful above all things and beyond cure. Who can understand it? I the Lord search the heart and examine the mind, to reward each person according to their conduct, according to what their deeds deserve" (Jeremiah 17:9–10).

It's easy to daydream about being admired and cared for. Our normal, wholesome desires only become sinful when our thoughts become obsessions, and we take matters into our hands. God wants to satisfy those desires in the right way and at the right time. When we give into temptation, we trade in God's best for a counterfeit. Instead of walking the road to wholeness according to his design, we deceive ourselves by believing a relationship will mend our hearts.

Instead of expecting another relationship to heal us, we must turn to the Healer. In the times we are weakest and most vulnerable, we must hold on to the Lord by deliberately and consistently turning our thoughts toward him. Memorizing scripture builds a wall of protection around our choices.

We've all heard the saying, "Time heals all wounds," but it's not true. Time *doesn't* heal all wounds. We can pretend it does, seek comfort in the arms of another, or self-medicate for temporal relief. None of these methods provide true relief from the pain and devastation of divorce.

The Search

Little girl searching;
Body of a woman wasting.
Tears shed as she is discarded once more,
Brokenhearted with her face to the floor.
Am I not worthy of love?
Her Maker weeps while she gives herself away;
Longing to heal the brokenness from the lack of embrace
Arms wide open, there he stands
With a precious rose in his hands.
You are beautiful my child, so dear to me
Come, let me show you what I created you to be.
I have made you precious with a beauty so rare
Not so that others can dampen your flair.
You are my daughter, a remarkable sight
A precious gem shimmering with gold.
My love for you is greater than you see
And your worth is found only in me.
I value you deeply and long for your love,
Take my hand and I'll lavish you with joy from above.
In me you are new
Trust, I'll show you what to do.
It's a new journey, one step at a time
Where you will find peace of mind.
Come as you are though tattered and bruised,
Come to me and I will make you anew.

The reflection you see is not what I planned.
With a renewed heart, your future is in my hands.
The acceptance and love you've sought all along
Is here in my arms, right where you belong
Come and receive the goodness in store
For you are not alone anymore.

The only one who can heal a broken heart from the inside out is Jesus. In order for him to do this, we have to trust him with our pain. We can't pretend we're not hurting and fake a smile for others to see. We can't crawl into our shell and block the world. Temptation is real and in the ruins of despair, anything that promises even temporary relief is enticing.

I felt the power of sexual temptations surrounding me. Sometimes when men approached me, I got a sinking feeling knowing their intentions were not good. Under normal circumstances resistance was easy, but because I was vulnerable, I considered straying from what was right. The self-destructive thoughts I fed gave way to increased guilt. Those sinful thoughts inflamed desire. If I continued to dwell on them, I would eventually act on them.

Game Plan

I understood that although my feelings were intense, they would be fleeting. My actions would remain, so I needed a game plan for my thoughts. I found the answer in this verse: "Finally, brethren, whatever things are true, whatever things are **noble**, whatever things are just, whatever things are **pure**, whatever things are **lovely**, whatever things are of good report, if there is any virtue and if there is anything praiseworthy—meditate on these things" (Philippians 4:8).

How can we mediate on pure, noble, and lovely things in a culture of sexual, violent, and grotesque images? This interior battle requires self-restraint and discipline. Whenever sexual thoughts or desires entered my mind, instead of contemplating them, I'd pray for God's help. I'd go over scriptures I'd memorized and reread the ones I'd marked in my Bible or written on note cards.

I decided to guard and protect my heart and do my part by remaining pure and transparent before the Lord. I earnestly wanted to do the will of God in my life and please him.

My countercultural choice puzzled people who didn't understand why I wasn't engaging in certain activities considered "normal" for a single person. I was ostracized. Yet, I continued my quest because God's opinion of me matters most.

Christ has given us instructions to overcome temptation. No one is immune, for even Christ himself was tempted. He lived in a human body and his greatest desire was to redeem his most treasured possession—us. He was laughed at, mocked, assaulted, and humiliated. The devil came at him full force to bring him down, but Christ remained pure. He never failed. Therefore, if I'm going to take advice from anyone on rising above temptation, it will be from him. In Matthew 26:41 (Amplified Bible) Jesus states: "All of you must **keep awake** and **watch** and **pray**, that you may not come into temptation. The spirit indeed is willing, but the flesh is weak."

First, *keep awake*. Give strict attention to the task, being cautious and active. We must take our Christian walk seriously and not be complacent in our faith. We must put forth effort to learn the ways of the Lord. When we love someone, we want to get to know them and spend time with them. Going to church, tithing and/or participating in church functions are all great, but they don't replace time learning and studying the Bible, and time spent in God's presence.

I fed my mind and spirit throughout the week. I read my Bible every morning and prayed throughout the day. I listened to Christian music and podcasts from several prominent pastors. These practices strengthened my faith, especially when I was discouraged.

Second, *watch*. Stay awake and mentally alert—to be on guard. We must remain on the lookout. Any of us can fall into temptation if we relax our vigilance. Although the Holy Spirit in us guides us to do the right thing, our flesh is weak. The things we secretly desire and focus on, we will do.

Third, *pray*. Prayer is communicating with God. The more we grow and mature in the Lord, the more sensitive we become to him. We'll discern his whispers in scripture and through reliable people. This all begins with prayer. Which scriptures help you pray and stand strong? Memorize or have them on hand for easy reference.

God does *not* tempt us because he is holy, and evil cannot entice him. We're tempted by our own desires. The slide into sin starts with our thoughts. The thoughts we feed become our desires. Those desires lead to actions and drag us down the slippery slope to destruction.

Thoughts → Desire → Sin →
Continuation of Sinful Lifestyle → Death

"Then, after desire has conceived, it gives birth to sin; and sin, when it is full-grown, gives birth to death" (James 1:15).

Take the First Step

Satan's greatest lie is that for God to forgive us, we must first change and become acceptable. It's simply not true. All he asks is for us to open our heart.

Jesus is the Bread of Life; without him human souls die of hunger. Everyone has a longing inside that only God can fill. Attempts to satisfy it with anything else including drugs, alcohol, food, sex, even academic or professional success, results in ongoing emptiness. Jesus loves us and waits with welcoming arms. He alone can give us the peace we desperately seek.

No one is perfect. Thankfully, God loves us just as we are and offers rest to our weary souls. "Then Jesus declared, I am the bread of life. He who comes to me will never go hungry, and he who believes in me will never go thirsty . . . whoever comes to me I will never drive away . . . This is the will of the one who sent me, I shall lose none of all that he has given me, but will raise them up at the last day" (John 6:35–39).

When we endure temptations, we rise above them. The pleasure of sin is temporary, but the reward of facing and resisting trials is the crown of life. Each and every time we choose not to succumb to temptation, we affirm, "Lord, I love you more than myself and I want to live my life to please you." When we receive this crown, we'll hear the beautiful words every follower of Christ longs for at the transition from death to eternal life, "Well done my good and faithful servant" (Matthew 25:23).

My Story

When I was seventeen I fell madly in love with "Mr. C." I had a crush on him for years before he noticed me. When he finally did, I was over the moon! We dated for several months and broke up when I caught him cheating. I was devastated. At church events, while attending with "her," he treated me like a stranger. I felt invisible and subhuman but said nothing and played along with the charade. Thinking I was foolish, I kept the pain to myself. That rejection haunted me for years, convincing me I was insignificant. I believed the lie, I didn't matter.

Years later, two days before my divorce was final, I ran into, you guessed it, Mr. C, who was still as handsome as ever. His face lit up when he saw me. He told me how beautiful I looked and that when we were together, he deeply cared for me. Then he asked if he could call me to "talk" because he was unhappy with his wife—the one he had dumped me for years earlier.

I had to run away from this situation—the day my seventeen-year-old-self had always imagined. My vindication arrived, "You see! You picked the wrong one!" This was the ultimate temptation. Satan knew my vulnerability, if I was going to fall it would have been with him. I had to consider my position as a child of God and example to my children and walk away. I put up my emotional guard and took steps to protect my mind, because my mind wanted to go to places that were not good.

I thought about that encounter for a long time and on several occasions caught myself regretting the decision to let him pass. My flesh wanted gratification. I wanted to be touched and be told I was important. I secretly fantasized about running into him again, but I knew this was wrong. He was someone else's husband. My thoughts were not pure before the Lord.

I am grateful I ran away from that encounter. Several years have passed and looking back at it, it would have been destructive. I couldn't see it at the time, but through this experience God tested my faith and I know it was his strength that sustained me.

Exchange temptation with endurance.

**TESTIMONY: BRENDA,
VICTORY FROM TEMPTATION**

My testimony of temptation started like the story of Job. I had everything I could have ever wanted. A house, a great job, and a marriage to a good Christian man, or so I thought. Then my husband left. I lost my job, my home, and my last companion, my dog. I went into a dark and lonely time.

From my childhood experiences of being molested and raped by an uncle and a female cousin, I believed sex was the only way to show and feel love. I drowned in the temptations that surrounded me.

Then I began to have feelings for a close friend who was married. He often asked me for advice about his relationship.

He respected me and made me feel loved and cared for. In my loneliness, he served as a comfort. The closer we became, the more I drifted from the Lord. I became increasingly attracted to him even though I knew my feelings were wrong.

I decided to be honest about my feelings and reached out to my pastor and some trusted friends. I'm thankful that the relationship never became sexual. Through my honesty, prayers, and the guidance I received, I was able to break free from him. It wasn't easy to leave his emotional support, something I longed for. I remember reciting "When I am weak Jesus You are strong" (2 Corinthians 12:9) and "I can do all things through Christ who gives me strength" (Philippians 4:13).

During this time, I worked my way back to God, although the painful path of loneliness continued. I brought people to the Lord and had friends again including a former female friend. It was wonderful. We went out to eat, did fun things together, and had a wonderful time, but I was unaware her intentions were different than mine.

We began to have feelings for each other which terrified me; I had been delivered from this over twenty years earlier. Once again God proved himself faithful when I would hear message after message about looking for love in all the wrong places. Many times, the Lord showed me his love and that I had to depend on Him. He knows the plans for my life, and I have to seek his kingdom and his righteousness above all things.

I know God's plans for me are good and he will continue to hold me up and deliver me from the evil that tries to bring me down. I have surrendered every desire to him and trust that he will continue to guide me on the path he has for me.

Temptations to stray from the Lord sexually bombard us in many ways. An old boyfriend. A new one. In our sex-saturated society, we face daily allurements to run to the nearest available arms to quench the loneliness that stalks divorced people. But with each verse we meditate on, each song of praise we sing internally or out loud, and each stand we take to trust Jesus and not fall to the enticement of the flesh, we find victory. Through it all we have the comfort that our new identity in Christ shines a bit brighter.

Christ gives us a new name:
VICTORIOUS.

CHAPTER SIX: TEMPTATION

Prayer

Lord, I pray you will cleanse my heart of all that is not of you. I want to honor you with every area of my life. Forgive me for the times I have failed you, (list specific areas). You promised there is no temptation that can overtake me (I Corinthians 10:13). I ask for your strength to overcome. Help me to be transparent with you, especially when my feelings try to overwhelm me. I want to be pure in spirit and in truth (Psalm 51:1–2) and not allow people, places, or things to rob the destiny you have for me. Help me to release all of the negative influences in my life and keep my mind focused on you.

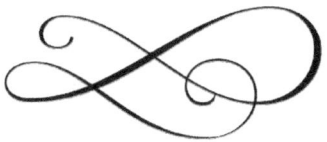

*"He restores my soul; He leads me
in the paths of righteousness for his name's sake."*

—Psalm 23:3

"Your word is a lamp for my feet, a light on my path."

—Psalm 119:105

Reflection

Before answering these questions, ask the Holy Spirit to bring to mind the areas of your life addressed in this chapter which need healing and change.

1.   What tempts you the most right now? What can you do to overcome it?

2.   When do your feelings overwhelm you? How do you cope?

3.   What part of your thought life do you need to surrender to God?

4. Which friendships or habits must go because they entice you to do the wrong things?

SEVEN

Forgiveness

A core tenet in the Christian faith is forgiveness. The Word of God is clear, to be forgiven we must forgive. "For if you forgive other people when they sin against you, your heavenly Father will also forgive you" (Matthew 6:14).

But . . .

- How can I forgive someone who has profoundly hurt me?

- How do I move past the anger?

- Is forgiveness a one-time event?

- What happens when someone continues hurting me?

- How do I forgive someone who purposely harms me?

Corrie Ten Boom's Example

Corrie Ten Boom and her family were devout Christians who lived out their faith by assisting underground efforts to save Jews from the Nazis during World War II. Corrie, her father, and her sister were subsequently arrested and imprisoned. Although she survived, both her beloved father and sister died in the concentration camps.

Instead of allowing these horrific experiences to cripple her with bitterness, Corrie used them as a catalyst to share the light and love of Jesus Christ. She wrote and traveled the world for the remainder of her life sharing her testimony.

During one of these speaking engagements, she came face to face with one of her greatest tormentors. He had humiliated Corrie and other prisoners in deplorable ways. Now this agent of torture stood in front of her with an outstretched arm—asking for her forgiveness.

She writes, *"And still I stood there with the coldness clutching my heart. But forgiveness is not an emotion—I knew that too. Forgiveness is an act of the will, and the will can function regardless of the temperature of the heart . . . 'Help!' I prayed silently. 'I can lift my hand. I can do that much. You supply the feeling.'*

"And so woodenly, mechanically, I thrust my hand into the one stretched out to me. And as I did, an incredible thing took place. The current started in my shoulder, raced down my arm, sprang into our joined hands. And then this healing warmth flooded my whole being, bringing tears to my eyes."

"'I forgive you, brother!' I cried. 'With all my heart!'

"For a long moment we grasped each other's hands, the former guard and the former prisoner. I had never known God's love so intensely, as I did then." Ten Boom, Corrie, John Sherrill, Sherrill, Elizabeth Sherrill. <u>The Hiding Place</u>. Ravensbrück, Netherlands: Barbour Books, 1971.

Corrie Ten Boom's example inspires me. The pain of my divorce was nothing compared to the horrors she faced. Her strength of character and faith encouraged me to look at my own life and identify the people I needed to forgive. If she forgave after what she went through, then certainly I could too.

What is Forgiveness?

Forgiveness acknowledges our hurt but surrenders the pain to God. It relinquishes attempts to control the situation and any desires or plans for retaliation. Forgiveness is not justifying the evil actions against us. Instead, it is the willful decision to no longer allow the past to dictate our happiness and future. *Forgiveness equals freedom.*

How Often Are We Supposed to Forgive?

Jesus' response is, "If your brother or sister sins against you, rebuke them; and if they repent, forgive them. Even if they sin against you seven times in a day and seven times come back to you saying, 'I repent,' you must forgive them." The apostles said to the Lord, "Increase our faith!" He replied, "If you have faith as small as a mustard seed, you can say to this mulberry tree, 'Be uprooted and planted in the sea,' and it will obey you" (Luke 17:4–6).

Notice the apostles' response to these instructions. "Increase our faith!" Why? Because it takes faith to forgive. We can't do it in our own strength. Jesus didn't say they needed more faith. He said with the little faith they had they could accomplish this task. Our *faith increases in proportion to our obedience.*

Just as the tiny mustard seed, when it's watered and cared for, becomes a huge, hardy tree, so our nurtured faith grows. As we continue this journey, each obedient step waters and strengthens that small seed. Eventually, we become unmovable, because we have learned to be totally dependent on God, fully assured that nothing is impossible for him.

Corrie Ten Boom knew all she needed to do was obey and trust the Lord. She took the first step as an act of faith and obedience. As she extended her hand, God supplied the rest.

Christ pointed to the mulberry, a tree that can withstand most adverse conditions. It grows quickly and may even survive after cutting the root; with only a little life left, it will regenerate. The only way to eliminate a mulberry tree is to *uproot* it, leaving no trace behind.

Similarly, if we hold on to small traces of unforgiveness, those remnants will spread quickly to every part of our lives, suffocating our future. It will steal our happiness and make us bitter and angry. Instead of peace, we'll ruminate on the past. This blocks forward movement.

Christ gives us the key, *uproot.* Uprooting is essential to obtaining freedom and healing from the prison of despair. With his authority we can command all traces of unforgiveness to depart from our lives.

Forgiveness is not denial. We must be honest and come to terms with our heartache. Our heavenly Father loves us and doesn't intend for us to live with the pain of trauma forever. History cannot be re-written, and memories will remain. However, with God's help and power, our difficult recollections can be transformed into tools of healing for others who have experienced similar tragedies.

Forgiveness is a choice and demands active faith. It might seem superficial because you might not feel it. Forgiveness can be instantaneous or gradual with ups and downs along the way. Learning to forgive doesn't demand perfection, just persistence. *If we purpose in our hearts to take that first step, God will give us the strength to forgive.* He knows our intentions and will help us in our weakness (2 Corinthians 12:9).

God recognizes how much you have been hurt and the burden you bear. He sees your anguish and how you long for the strength to forgive, but don't know how. When we are honest and surrender our will, he takes the lead and gives us the grace to do those things we never thought possible.

What if They Don't Take Responsibility?

Forgiveness isn't always a two-way street. We can choose to forgive those who hurt us even if they don't take responsibility for their actions. They may never acknowledge what they did or said; we may never get the apology we desire. The offenders may never care enough to understand the magnitude of the repercussions of their actions.

We can also choose to forgive without knowing all the facts. Initially, I only knew part of the reason why my former spouse didn't want to reconcile. As time went on, I knew I had to let go and allow healing in my heart. I forgave him and surrendered it all before the Lord.

Over a year after the final divorce decree, I discovered more of the secret life he lived during our marriage. The heartbreaking information brought all my pain back. Two years of growth seemed to go down the drain. Part of me wanted to renege on the forgiveness I extended and reclaim my anger. When the truth about his past emerged, memories and insecurities overwhelmed my mind.

Rather than let the past imprison me again, I decided to forgive—wanting to remain free. I trusted God to help me, and he did.

Christ forgave us before we asked. Knowing what lay ahead of him, Jesus moved forward, albeit in anguish. His physical pain and spiritual torture were greater than we can conceive. Aware he was about to experience the fullness of God's wrath, hell, separation from the Father, abandonment, and physical torture at the hands of those he loved, he willingly placed himself on the sacrificial altar. He forgave the very ones who spat, mocked, whipped, humiliated, and betrayed him saying, "Father, forgive them, for they do not know what they are doing" (Luke 23:34a).

Instead of saving himself, he saved us.

How mysterious are God's ways? How often have we figured out how situations should unfold and become spiteful and angry when we don't get our way? God has a bigger plan than any of us can imagine. If he did not spare his Son, but crushed him for our benefit, is there anything he won't do for our salvation? He gave us the ultimate gift, but at times we discard it with disdain. How it must crush the heart of our Savior every time we disgrace his sacrifice, every time we turn our backs on him to follow our selfish pleasures and ambitions.

When we accept Christ's forgiveness, we are reconciled to him. Christ enables us to forgive every person who hurts us. We need to humbly ask him to help. He knows the uphill road it has been. We must be honest with him about our feelings. Confession may feel awkward at first, but if we are willing to learn and grow, God will carry us on this journey.

Release the past and choose forgiveness.

TESTIMONY: SHERRY,
DIVORCED AFTER A TWO-YEAR MARRIAGE

Graduate high school . . . check, graduate college . . . check, obtain a degree and establish a career . . . check, check! Now the next step . . . find a life partner and start a family.

I met a wonderful person. Our thrilling relationship meant I was no longer alone. I had my life partner, a companion to make new memories and have experiences with. The next year, in the presence of family and friends, we married. Our beautiful beginning felt like a fairy tale.

I'm a social butterfly and very close to family. Little by little my husband expressed anger over my friendships. He began to control who I could visit and welcome to our home.

On September 15th at 12:05p.m., I gave birth to a beautiful, healthy baby boy—the happiest day of my life. Announcements went out via phone calls to all our family and friends. I hoped the birth of our son would help smooth things out, but instead my husband's demands and exclusions got worse. He was openly hostile and verbally aggressive to my friends and family.

One day he asked if I was happy with our life together and if I would like to have another child. When I hesitated, he shouted "You f***ing whore!" He repeated those venomous words as he charged toward me.

I reacted by slapping his face. He began hitting me. Lying in a fetal position, I begged him to stop. When he finally released me, he headed toward our son. With a malicious grin, he raised his hand and shushed me. Fearing for my son's life, I called 9-1-1. I knew he had a bad temper, but never imagined he was capable of this.

Difficult months followed. I had no job or money. He cut off my phone and all access to credit cards and bank accounts. If it wasn't for my family, especially my sister, I don't know how I would have survived.

Ten years after my divorce I still harbored hatred towards him. I blamed him for all the feelings I had and claimed he was the one that made me bitter and angry.

The happier I heard he was, the more I resented him. Even the sound of his name made me uneasy. Every time I saw a picture of him and his wife, fury arose in me.

I told a coworker about my feelings. She reached over and grabbed my hands saying, "Let's pray. You need to free yourself from this. Unforgiveness has kept you in bondage far too long. You have to forgive and let it go."

I looked at her and became overwhelmed with emotions. One part of me agreed. The other part thought 'Hell no. He doesn't deserve my forgiveness. He needs to ask me for it!'

We went to an unoccupied room. She clenched my hands and prayed over me. I wanted to forgive and no longer let hatred control my life. When I tried to speak forgiveness, I couldn't. It felt as if my mouth was being covered. I cried out and felt my knees buckle.

That night I remember saying as I fell asleep "God, I don't know what to do or how to do it . . . I don't want to feel like this anymore."

A few weeks later I was invited to church. The teaching was on forgiveness—a direct hit to the heart. The pastor said, "It's been a long time since you have been holding on to that, let it go, just let it go." Tears streamed down my face. My girlfriend gripped my hand and encouraged me to go to the altar for healing. I told her I couldn't. I felt heavy and unable to move. But I went.

I fell to my knees and cried uncontrollably. The pastor instructed me to repeat a prayer after him and I did proclaiming, "In the name of our beloved Jesus and God Almighty, I release the bond of unforgiveness, and I choose to forgive my ex-husband. I have forgiven all wrongdoing and walk in peace from this day forward." He continued to repeat it and I followed, repeating the words louder and stronger. A weightless sensation of joy rushed over and filled me. I got up and praised God for setting me free.

At that moment, I realized forgiveness was the catalyst for my freedom. I think about that day often and thank God for bringing the right people into my life to help me move forward. I still have difficult encounters with my ex-husband, but instead of them bringing me into a place of bondage and anger, I pray and seek God for guidance and strength.

Part of our renewed identity in Christ is walking in the courage to choose forgiveness, instead of letting wounded emotions, feelings, control us. Christ enables us to do this even when we receive no apology or acknowledgement of remorse from the offender. Like Corrie Ten Boom, we will experience God's empowerment and overwhelming love when by faith we forgive.

Christ gives us a new name:
FREE.

CHAPTER SEVEN: FORGIVENESS

Prayer

Lord, I want to be obedient to you and walk in forgiveness, but I don't know how. Help me. Although I don't feel it, I will take the first step in obedience to you, knowing you will carry me through. In the name of Jesus, I break all the chains of unforgiveness and renounce its power over my life. I choose to forgive name of person(s). I no longer want to live in the prison of despair. Thank you for my freedom! Help me to see name of person(s) through your eyes. Help me to love like you. Help me to obey you. I have faith that with your help I can do anything, including this. Thank you, Lord. I pray all of this in Jesus' name. Amen.

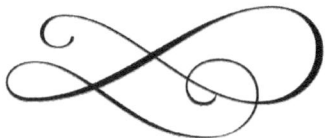

"Blessed is the one whose transgressions are forgiven, whose sins are covered. Blessed is the one whose sin the Lord does not count against and in whose spirit is no deceit. When I kept silent, my bones wasted away through my groaning all day long. For day and night your hand was heavy on me; my strength was sapped as in the heat of summer. Then I acknowledged my sin to you and did not cover up my iniquity. I said, "I will confess my transgressions to the Lord." And you forgave the guilt of my sin. Therefore let all the faithful pray to you while you may be found; surely the rising of the mighty waters will not reach them. You are my hiding place; you will protect me from trouble and surround me with songs of deliverance."

—Psalm 32:1–7

Reflection

Before answering these questions, ask the Holy Spirit to bring to mind the areas of your life addressed in this chapter which need healing and change.

1.   Who have you been unable to forgive?

2.   What beliefs about forgiveness block you from forgiving?

3.   Are there people you think you have forgiven, but instantly resent when they offend you again? How has the information in this chapter equipped you to overcome the renewed resentment?

EIGHT

Pure In Heart

J was convinced I had completely forgiven my former spouse. I made conscious efforts to not speak ill of him and tried my best to be pleasant during child exchanges. Yet, whenever someone initiated a conversation about my divorce or asked probing questions, I defended myself, making sure those around me knew "it wasn't *my* fault." I didn't want others to like him because in my mind that meant *I* was defective.

Although I had forgiven him, I still carried the baggage of anger and resentment. While forgiveness was part of the solution, I needed to take another step. I had to *be pure in heart.*

What Does That Mean?

Forgiveness is a choice. Purity of heart is the evidence of that choice. It involves monitoring our thoughts, words, and deeds. A person with a pure heart will strive to speak the truth in love and not out of anger and bitterness. But truth in love does not mean rolling over and letting someone walk on you. It means examining our motives before we speak and making sure we're not reacting out of retaliation or vindication.

It is the act of blessing those that curse us.

We avoid opportunities to gossip about a former spouse or his family. Most people think they have done their part by not speaking ill of that person in front of their children. While that's true, it's *not* enough. Gossip about a former spouse demonstrates our own lack of healing and surrender. Refraining from unkind words is hard. A restrained tongue is the greatest hurdle to master but rewards us with the keys to ultimate freedom. "Out of the abundance of the heart the mouth speaks" (Luke 6:45). "Instead, speaking the truth in love, we will grow to become in every respect the mature body of him who is the head, that is, Christ" (Ephesians 4:15).

Many inhibit their healing by staying stuck in anger, because like me, they falsely assure themselves they have forgiven. Shallow forgiveness is short lived. Just as a leopard cannot change his spots, neither will a former spouse change his behavior. We should not be surprised when someone acts in line with their character. We should expect it and not allow anger and bitterness to choke out godly reactions.

A pure heart lacks hypocrisy or hidden motives. A transparent person desires to please God with more than an outward show of good behavior. Purity of heart penetrates the soul.

To have this, we must determine to turn over our lives to Jesus and ask him to cleanse us. Psalm 51:10 says, "Create in me a pure heart, O God, and renew a steadfast spirit within me." God makes our hearts pure by the sacrifice of his Son and through his sanctifying work in our lives (1 John 3:1–3).

Conflict

Former spouses can press our buttons better than anyone else. They know our weaknesses and insecurities and at times their words stab like daggers and cut us to the core. Hurtful or sarcastic comments serve as a catalyst for ongoing feuds. Past resentments creep in and further erode a deteriorated relationship. The reality is some people don't know how to move past the conflict and aren't interested in investing the mental and emotional energy required to overcome it.

Walking in forgiveness, insight, and meaningful communication are critical to unraveling the roots of conflict.

- Forgiveness: Forgiveness is an ongoing choice.

- Insight: Often we see ourselves as victims and fail to recognize how we contribute to conflict. Honesty hurts but is necessary. Being true to ourselves and understanding our underlying motivations is a crucial step in self-awareness. Many people fall by the wayside in this arduous process and never succeed. Once we commit to identifying our own failures and selfish ambitions, we better understand how our interactions affect others.

- Meaningful Communication: The patterns we have developed over the years will either help or hinder our interactions. Communication between you and your former spouse can be complicated. There may be difficulty listening and understanding each other because of your long history of preconceived notions and the baggage of the relationship. We must actively engage and listen to try to understand what the other person is saying before we respond.

- Preparation: You know what your spouse or ex-spouse tends to think, say, and do. With that knowledge in mind, plan your words and actions to be Christlike. Commit to listening. Restrict yourself to only discussing issues, not emotions or criticisms.

The above requires discipline, practice, and taking active steps to avoid angry and bitter reactions. My first steps on the road to purity of heart were calculated. Whenever I had to encounter my former husband, I practiced the scenario in my head several times beforehand. I resisted opportunities for revenge, even when I had some great zingers that would've really gotten to him.

Sometimes I regretted not saying them because I thought they were really funny. Other times I would zing him and laugh hysterically at his expense. In hindsight, my childish antics were a poor choice intended to hurt his feelings. By repaying evil with evil I demonstrated how much I still wanted to humiliate him. Those passive aggressive actions banished peace.

At times, our interactions went well and other times they didn't. I studied the pitfalls and practiced emotional detachment. This kept me from having my day ruined. I prayed about it and asked God to give me wisdom in the future.

Although retaliating may feel good in the moment, we should instead plan ways to do good (Proverbs 25:22). This is easier said than done and can only be accomplished through the power of God.

Praying for Your Former Spouse

"But I say to you, love your enemies and pray for those who persecute you" (Matthew 5:44).

The scripture says to not only pray for, but to *love* our *enemies*.

So, what does that look like?

To love your enemies means we overcome evil with good. We treat them with respect, whether they deserve it or not and, most importantly, we pray for God's grace, mercy, and goodness for them. It doesn't mean going back into a relationship with this person.

Sometimes we will face difficult situations that can only be resolved through fasting and prayer. For me this was one. I would fast for days at a time. Some were partial fasts where I abstained from certain types of food and entertainment. Others were full fasts when I would not eat and spent my time in prayer and reading the Bible. In these fasts, I prayed for my former husband, not for our reconciliation, but for his soul. I wanted God to equip me with the strength needed to carry out his mandate. "Blessed are the pure in heart for they will see God" (Matthew 5:8).

God has been faithful through this painful process and as much as I didn't understand it at the time, I chose to obey.

Through prayer and fasting, God began a restorative work in my heart. I began to feel differently about my former husband. Pity replaced my desire to retaliate. I started to see him as a lost brother who needed to reconcile his life with God and wanted him to experience freedom in Christ.

The struggle continues. There are times I still want to engage aggressively and mirror his reactions or one-up him. Most people would accept that reaction because there's no expiration date on the wounds he inflicted. But as a child of God I am called to a higher standard. I have to trust and obey God even when I don't feel like it.

Just as God asks us to forgive those who have hurt us, he also asks that we walk in purity of heart, as this is the only way to experience true freedom from the events that hold us captive.

Exchange resentment for purity of heart.

TESTIMONY: EMMA,
HAPPILY MARRIED AFTER A DIFFICULT DIVORCE

They say men in midlife crisis either get a motorcycle, a sports car, or a younger woman. After twenty years of marriage my husband opted for a younger woman. It was by far the most painful event in my life. We were both ministers in our church.

He grew increasingly distant. I ignored the signs he was drifting from me, because I assumed losing his love could never happen.

One day the reality I had long denied surfaced. He left on a Thanksgiving and never returned. I was blindsided. My family was devastated. I suspected another woman was involved and asked God to show me the truth. I found the evidence I needed and confronted him. He denied it. I wanted my marriage to work so I asked him to choose between me or her.

He continued to deny his extra marital affair and thus began the worst nightmare of my life. When you ask God to show you truth the lights turn on and everything starts to make sense. I found things around the house that uncovered his secret life of pornography, lust, and adultery.

His continuous lies and double life put me through hell. Yet, through it all—I still loved him. I couldn't help my feelings or numb the pain. I knew he was with another woman, yet I couldn't let him go.

I fought for my marriage and spent an entire year praying, fasting, and interceding for our reconciliation. Unfortunately, he was saying one thing to me and doing another. He would say he was sorry and that he would leave it all behind, that he would fight for our family. However, his actions demonstrated the exact opposite.

My children felt stressed when he used our home as a revolving door. Some weeks he was home, others he was gone. He undermined their stability and became a stranger.

My children and I clung to the false hope he would change. Their dashed hopes turned to rage and caused them to question their faith and God's love.

Through the rollercoaster of emotions, I made one crucial decision. I decided to forgive and pursue a pure heart toward him. I never spoke badly about him, and I encouraged my children to have a relationship with their father. Looking back,

I know it was only by God's grace that I was able to do this. The anger my children carried toward him was crippling.

A couple of years after our divorce, he was diagnosed with cancer. After a difficult battle, he passed away. Through his fight against cancer, my children were there for him every step of the way, something they could not have done if they had not overcome their resentment. I was also able to provide care and demonstrate the love of Jesus in his deepest time of need.

I would not have been able to do any of those things or be of support to my children without pure motives toward my former husband. Almighty God enabled me to do this through the gift of his strength in my life.

Exchanging the natural inclination for resentment and receiving a heart that forgives and lips that speak blessing, enables us to live victoriously when the heartache of divorce would beat us down. Like Emma shared in her testimony, our reliance on our mighty God strengthens us. Our strength in him is a catalyst to also remove the pain and resentment our children feel and help them walk into God's power and light.

Christ gives us a new name:
PURE IN HEART.

CHAPTER EIGHT: PURE IN HEART

Prayer

Lord, I know I will not be able to move forward into the wholeness you have for me if I carry resentment. I ask you to show me the areas of my life where I have not walked in purity of heart to those around me. Remove all critical and judgmental attitudes and replace them with a tenderness of heart. I struggle with this, and it has kept me bound. I pray you will teach me daily how to walk with a pure heart, especially toward those who have hurt me. I want to see and experience a deeper walk with you. Take my hand Lord, as I want to reflect your beauty and grace in all areas of my life.

"Create in me a pure heart, O God,
and renew a steadfast spirit within me"

—*Psalm 51:10*

"Who may ascend the mountain of the Lord? Who may stand in his holy
place? The one who has clean hands and a pure heart, who does not
trust in an idol or swear by a false god. They will receive blessing from
the Lord and vindication from God their Savior. Such is the generation
of those who seek him, who seek your face, God of Jacob."

—*Psalm 24:3–6*

Reflection

Before answering these questions, ask the Holy Spirit to bring to mind the areas of your life addressed in this chapter which need healing and change.

1. What action steps can you take to walk in purity of heart toward your former spouse?

2. Do you find it hard not to speak ill of your former spouse? What are some ways you can bless him with your words?

3. Are you an active participant in a conflicted relationship with your former spouse? If yes, what are some ways you contribute to the conflict? What can you do to change the dynamic?

NINE

Count It All Joy?

Let's revisit the life of John the Baptist. We saw how his life ended, but now let's go back to the beginning. Elizabeth and Zechariah dreamt of having a son, but as the years of barrenness continued, they lost hope. Elizabeth likely felt a sting similar to the emptiness of divorce. She saw other families "complete" and full of joy. In her heart she knew she would be a good mother, as many of us know we were good wives. I'm sure a little piece of her heart broke every time she saw a pregnant woman, or a young child cradle his mother's neck. That must have been a constant reminder of what she longed for but didn't have.

Then one day, her husband came home, mute. He wrote down a message he received from an angel. The Bible says the angel told him his prayers had been answered! As impossible as it seemed God answered their prayer in a way they never imagined. The message was clear—Elizabeth *would* have a son. *Finally*, God would fulfill her dream. Her family would be complete.

John was the long-awaited answer. While they waited, God prepared Elizabeth and Zechariah to be the perfect parents for this man of great purpose, by polishing their faith over many years. If they had known how their beloved's son life would end do you think they would have asked God to reconsider?

God doesn't give us all the answers. Many times, he asks us to take one step at a time, moving us closer to his will. John's life was destined for a purpose far beyond anything he or his parents could've imagined. Even his death glorified God, a silent message to the king that God would not be mocked.

It was a living reminder—we must follow through and do what is right, no matter the cost.

"Consider it pure joy, my brothers and sisters, whenever you face trials of many kinds, because you know that the testing of your faith produces perseverance. Let perseverance finish its work so that you may be mature and complete, not lacking anything. If any of you lacks wisdom, you should ask God, who gives generously to all without finding fault, and it will be given to you. But when you ask, you must believe and not doubt, because the one who doubts is like a wave of the sea, blown and tossed by the wind. That person should not expect to receive anything from the Lord. Such a person is double-minded and unstable in all they do" (James 1:2–8).

What Does This Mean?

So, what does it mean to "count it all joy?" It means when our world is falling apart, we don't focus on ourselves, but on eternity with the Lord. We keep the big picture in mind, knowing that God is with us and will help us through any situation. It doesn't mean to put on a fake smile, act phony, and pretend we're not struggling.

In the midst of trials, we rarely comprehend the big questions: how, when, and why? We may never understand because our wisdom is finite.

Counting it all joy means:

- Having faith that no matter the outcome, God will help us through.

- Remembering God knows the end from the beginning, and he will work every situation for the good, even if we don't see it in our lifetime.

- Knowing God can use our struggles to reach others. The challenges we overcome can be great lessons for those who experience similar situations.

Our greatest trials and tests of faith can either make or break us. How we respond during the most challenging situations can be the difference between life and death.

During difficult times do we:

- Find ourselves filled with anxiety?

- Isolate?

- Revert to old behavior patterns?

- Pray and when we don't see immediate change or God doesn't respond the way we want, give up and become despondent to him?

Or

- Do we seek the Lord for his guidance in how to move forward?

- Make him our refuge?

- Go to him with our pain, weakness, and suffering?

- Seek encouragement from godly men and women?

Christian Maturity

When we are tested and our faith prevails, our patience increases. With more patience, we navigate stressful situations and difficulties without anger or irritation. This is a mark of Christian maturity. When we're patient, we're better equipped to allow God to deal with the problem or person instead of trying to fix things, only to frustrate ourselves.

Our trials teach us to depend on the Lord. When we finally learn the lesson "to let go and let God," we get better at surrendering every situation to him, knowing he will guide our responses. Sometimes he prompts us to speak, and at other times, to keep silent.

Some of our trials are the result of our own actions. The Lord may also allow other challenges to develop our character. Either way, the longer we worry, try to influence the outcome, and blame God, the more difficult the trial will be. Trying to control a situation and seeing no change will inevitably lead to hopelessness.

When we persevere through a trial and see the hand of God operate in our lives, our faith grows. As we increase in faith, we mature and our trust in him increases. "Let perseverance finish its work so that you may be mature and complete, not lacking anything" (James 1:4).

- Mature: During difficult situations, we experience God's care in our lives and our faith is increased. When difficulties come, we have complete assurance God will be with us. We are steadfast, unmovable, and unshakeable.

- Complete: We are full, whole. Unaddressed pain causes us to live as a fractured person. This could be a result of a variety of issues: childhood trauma, poor decisions, betrayal, rejection, insecurities, illness, death, adult trauma, and the divorce process. The enemy of our soul uses those shattered parts as triggers to bring us into condemnation, guilt, and depression. Once we address those areas, we can relinquish them to the Lord. Confronting and surrendering the pain invites God to begin the healing process in our lives.

- Lacking nothing: We lack nothing. When we surrender our lives completely to God, we can live to our greatest potential. Those areas that held us back become the stepping-stones of our future. We are free to live life in peace, despite our demanding situations and have the blessed assurance that we are in God's hands.

This may seem farfetched, especially when nothing around us makes sense. Although we may not understand now, we must trust that while our life may be in ruins, God loves us and will help us through.

During trying times, trusting God may be difficult. We've all had moments of doubt. Instead of pretending nothing is wrong, talk to the Lord. He already knows what we are feeling and thinking. Masking doubt is dangerous. We may pretend to be strong to the outside world, but inside we're telling God:

- I can't trust you.
- I know what's best.
- There is no way you can help me.

This process is insidious. First, we doubt. Then we begin to justify actions and/or thoughts we know are wrong. Then little by little we justify and rationalize old behaviors and coping patterns that bring relief and escape.

Things will not always go the way we want. In spite of this, we must continue, and have faith to believe God has a perfect plan for our lives, even when we cannot see it.

Jochebed (Exodus 1 and 2)

Our perspective about the apparent unfairness of life is finite and limited. When we see no hope, we feel paralyzed and depressed. Many biblical accounts describe similar situations. Let's consider Jochebed.

Jochebed was Moses' mother. Much emphasis is placed on Moses and how he led the Israelites to an awesome victory. However, in order to win, he and his family of origin overcame great adversity. Jochebed had three strikes against her: she was a woman, a Hebrew, and a slave. In other words, in that society, she was the lowest of the low.

When Moses was born, the people of Israel were slaves in Egypt. Although treated cruelly, they thrived and increased in number. This threatened the Egyptian ruler. Attempting to control the growing population and destroy the spirit of the people, Pharaoh instituted a law to kill all male Hebrew babies.

Then the worst-case scenario happened—Jochebed became pregnant. As a mother, I can only imagine her dread when she found out. We can presume she prayed during those months when we look back on the history of the nation her son grew to lead.

Finally, her baby was born—a boy. What fear must have consumed this family as they came to terms with the reality that their newest member was doomed to death.

"And she became pregnant and gave birth to a son. When she saw that he was a fine child, she hid him for three months. But when she could hide him no longer, she got a papyrus basket for him and coated it with tar and pitch. Then she placed the child in it and put it among the reeds along the bank of the Nile" (Exodus 2:2–3).

Jochebed didn't let the edict of a vicious king squelch her hope. When she looked at Moses, she knew he was special. As a loving mother, she decided to hide her child. For a brief time, her efforts seemed futile. Every cry endangered the family, calling attention to their defiance of a government ruling.

All seemed hopeless. Surrounded by an evil culture, there was little she could do. Who was she? What power did a Hebrew slave wield? What difference could she make?

I believe Jochebed prayed for a plan to save her baby despite the law of the land. She acted in faith in the midst of the impossibility of her situation. She waterproofed a basket, tucked a blanket around her beloved son and gently launched the little ark into the Nile River. With nothing left, she walked away. What pain must have gripped her heart as she placed her precious baby in the treacherous Nile?

Then the unimaginable happened! Pharaoh's daughter came to that very spot in the river to bathe and spotted the basket. She opened it and saw the baby crying. Moved by pity and love, she decided to adopt him as her own. At that moment Moses went from Hebrew slave with a death sentence, to an Egyptian prince with servants for protection.

Moses' older sister Miriam, still a child herself, courageously stayed nearby to watch over him. She approached the princess, risking her life, to offer a suitable woman to nurse the child. Jochebed was able to keep Moses and nurse him in safety. She no longer feared for his life. He was now under the protection of Pharaoh himself.

When faced with evil, Jochebed chose to act against it. At first, her plan with a little basket seemed unobtainable and absurd, but God used her efforts and courage for a plan greater than she ever imagined. When we focus on the impossibility of our situation, we become paralyzed and stagnate in fear and dread. When we focus on God, we move forward trusting him for the resolution.

"Are not two sparrows sold for a penny? Yet not one of them will fall to the ground outside your Father's care. And even the very hairs of your head are all numbered. So don't be afraid; you are worth more than many sparrows" (Matthew 10:29–31).

God knows everything we have endured and will endure. We are in his care, and he has not forgotten us. I marvel over the part of the verse that says he knows every hair on our heads. During my divorce, I lost a significant amount of hair, grieving as it fell out in chunks. For a while I had a bald spot on the top of my head the size of a baseball. Because I have thick hair, I was able to hide that loss from others. I was ashamed. I prayed this verse over my situation. Knowing that I was in his care, even when my world was broken and my hair was falling out, gave me peace.

Your experiences will differ from mine. Your story may be more complicated, but one thing we have in common is the knowledge that in Christ there is fullness of joy and peace. It's only when we surrender our shattered lives to him, that he can help us overcome every depression and tension. Although God's rescue does not always come the way we expect, we can rest assured he has not forgotten us.

Exchange hopelessness with assurance.

TESTIMONY: LYNETA SMITH,
HAPPILY REMARRIED AFTER A DIFFICULT DIVORCE

Another sleepless night. I tucked my children who were seven and four, into their bunk beds and braced for silence to fill our tiny apartment. Five a.m. would come far too quickly, but like so many nights before, sweet dreams would elude me.

Daily worries about the girls' emotions and how I would pay the rent morphed into giants. Alone, I allowed them to torment me because I had nowhere to go for shelter. I couldn't go to God—he was too angry with me.

I still determined to raise my little girls to know him, but every struggle I had as a single parent confirmed I'd lost favor with God. On Sundays, I dressed the girls in cute dresses and toted them to church. While they were in their Sunday school class, I sat in the back pew. Avoiding any deep relationships meant avoiding judgment, so I barely knew anyone there.

My previous church had been my sole source of friends. As a stay-at-home mom, before I escaped my first husband, I volunteered as a children's ministry worker, participated in a home school group, and attended Bible studies. Leaving meant cutting off my entire social support network.

The elders were clear about marriage and divorce. Anyone who left a spouse was subject to church discipline, which meant eventual excommunication. When I sought counsel, a revered older woman gave me this advice regarding my physically abusive husband: "Just make sure you do everything your husband asks, then you won't get hurt."

I'd tried. What the well-meaning lady and the elders didn't understand about domestic violence is an abuser doesn't need a reason. Sometimes, there's nothing a battered wife can do to prevent a blowup. I kept thinking, "If only I can be a good enough wife, then he'll love me." Hard as I tried, I could never be good enough.

I stopped trying the day I witnessed him striking our oldest daughter in a rage. "I may deserve this, but they don't," I thought. Even if it meant risking my eternal damnation, I would not allow them to live in physical danger.

Though I'd achieved physical freedom, day-to-day struggles still weighed me down. Financially, I lived on the edge. Whether I had a sick child or a broken-down car, I always stressed about too little money or time. I couldn't take my worries to God, not after I disobeyed the church elders and left my husband. One of the pastors and a few members of the congregation even sent me letters telling me to return and repent "before it's too late."

I didn't miss my church friends or my ex-husband, but I did miss feeling connected with God. If only I could talk to him—not to ask for anything, just to be with him.

One day I dusted off my Bible, opened to Psalms, and read for the first time in months. David's sorrow over his sin pierced my heart. I thought about all the other people's lives recorded in the Word—Moses, Abraham, Peter—every one of them had made life-changing errors, yet still had favor with God.

I slid off the couch and onto my knees, then bowed my head and clasped hands. "God, I know you're mad at me. I don't even know if you're listening, but I can't do this thing alone. If you could just show me the way back to you."

The God Who Sees (Genesis 16:13) looked down on me, a broken, fearful young woman and reaffirmed that he will never leave me or forsake me (Hebrews 13:5), No matter how many times I messed up, he assured me that he loved me unconditionally (Romans 8:35, I John 4:9–10), his grace covers all that I have done (Ephesians 2:8).

From then on, I didn't view every financial crisis or single-parent challenge as God's punishment. Knowing God was with me gave me the courage to eventually move from the back pew to the choir loft, but in the meantime, I could rejoice in the days he'd given me. I had my joy back.

Those outside of Christ find it hard to comprehend that we can rejoice in our trials. We can because we have precious promises of God's provision and presence. The book of James exhorts us to count it *all* joy. In our hardest times, Jesus continues to shape us - saved, forgiven, and filled with the power and love of God himself. Keeping the words of scripture in our minds enables us to walk no longer as a D for divorced but a C—in Christ.

Christ gives us a new name:
UNSHAKEABLE.

CHAPTER NINE: COUNT IT ALL JOY?

Prayer

Lord, your Word says you give rest to the weary and heavy laden (Matthew 11:28–30). I am discouraged and feel disillusioned by the way my life has turned out. You alone know the weight of the burdens I carry. I need your help Lord. Your Word says that you are a present help in times of trouble (Psalm 46:1). I need that help today. I come to the throne of grace to receive your healing touch. I place every broken dream at your feet including (list the areas of your life where you are disappointed). I give each of these to you and choose to trust you in spite of what I see. I have faith to know that nothing is too difficult for you (Luke 1:37). Be my refuge, my strong tower, and my peace in the midst of the storms of my life (Psalm 9:9). Strengthen my heart and build up my faith so I will have the patience to wait on you (Psalm 27:1–4). Thank you Lord for you will again revive me (Psalm 71:20–21).

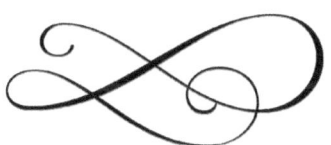

"As for me, I call to God, and the Lord saves me.
Evening, morning and noon I cry out in distress, and he hears my voice. He
rescues me unharmed from the battle waged against me,
even though many oppose me."

Psalm 55:16–18

Reflection

Before answering these questions, ask the Holy Spirit to bring to mind the areas of your life addressed in this chapter which need healing and change.

1. Do you ever find yourself pretending to be "okay" when inside you feel like you are about to fall apart?

2. What is your first response when you encounter difficult situations?

3. What current situations discourage you? What old patterns of behavior are you tempted to revert to?

4. How often are you bringing your concerns to God? What areas of your angst, questions, and doubts are hardest to be honest about in prayer? List them and take the time to remember the Lord loves you and watches over you with care.

TEN

Children

othing is nearer and dearer to our hearts than our children, God's gift to us. Few parents would intentionally inflict harm. However, during and after divorce, our children suffer more than we do.

Divorce traumatizes children. It's the death of their family, the end of the only life they know. We must ask God for strength to love our children through this difficult process. They need us more than ever in order to dispel the lies Satan wants them to believe.

As parents, it is our responsibility to guide our children through their emotional upheavals despite our own distress. By seeking God and allowing him to heal our wounded hearts, we will find strength to offer hope to our children.

As a wife, I struggled with feelings of abandonment, rejection, and anguish. As a mother, those feelings were compounded when I realized my children would grow up in a broken home. With God's help, I needed to break the cycle.

Fear

What is a child's greatest fear? The death of one or both of their parents. In a similar way, a child's worldview is damaged by divorce. The stability they once knew is gone as they move to new homes and/or navigate between two homes. Finances change, usually diminishing, and while they may have lived with dysfunctional patterns, that was their normal.

Their world has been turned upside down and a new normal must be established. During this transition, many become preoccupied with the thought that if they are separated from a certain parent, that parent might die.

Children express stress and anxiety differently than adults. If we, as a parent, struggle to express our emotions, our children struggle more. Their pent-up feelings manifest in other ways. Signs of childhood anxiety can include excessive separation anxiety, worry about being kidnapped, increased bed-wetting, and nightmares. Children may also become despondent or may experience physical ailments such as increased stomachaches and headaches.

Protection of the Other Parent

Children love and need both parents. When one is absent, a child may try to protect that parent from the verbal insults or insinuations of others. Additionally, they often build up illusions of grandeur about the absentee parent. This stems from the ego's need to protect itself because no one ever wants to believe they are unwanted.

As a social worker, I've seen children that have been removed from their homes by the state due to parental abuse. Even when placed in a loving foster home, the children still felt a loyalty to their family of origin. It's the "missing link," a part of their identity. When one parent demeans and disparages the other, they are putting down the child, because that parent is a part of them. No amount of rationalizing will change this. It's an element of the human spirit. We all want to belong, to feel special, and loved. Children seek this from *both* their parents.

Wanting Parents to Reconcile

Children often blame themselves for their parents' conflicts. They mistakenly believe if they are good enough mommy and daddy will get back together. Because of this, many try to orchestrate reconciliation. They may invent ways for parents to be in the same room together and after failed attempts to initiate reconnection, become despondent. Even years after the divorce, many carry a glimmer of hope that one day their parents will reunite.

Be honest with your children and explain they played no role in causing the divorce, so they can accept the truth they can't put it back together. Reassure them they are loved and seek help from outside sources as well. Youth pastors, supportive family members, and professional counselors can provide needed support.

We *must* validate the pain our children suffer because of the divorce. Take the time to listen. Hold them when they cry. Cry with them. Let them know you are hurting too, and this is not easy for you. They need you. Be there for them and reaffirm your love.

When pain remains unacknowledged, children learn to mistrust their emotional barometer. This mistrust carries into adulthood as they navigate other relationships. They will assume their feelings aren't important and they should just get over it, which is *never a good idea*. As they mature, they will be unable to cope with other issues that come up and may be stuck in "arrested development" for years to come, because they were never given the room to grieve.

Parenting

A central issue for parents involves redefining emotional boundaries and identity, particularly in the family roles. Initially, divorcees often feel less effective in performing their family and other life roles.

In addition to severing the spousal relationship, divorce also affects the couple's interactions and the way they fulfill their parental functions. As a result, these roles must be reconstructed. If parents are unable to communicate effectively on behalf of their children post-divorce, strain between the children and the parents will result.

Children need both parents. A mountain of published research explains this. God created both mother and father. Even when parents live separately, it's important for both to have ample time with the children without interference from the other parent.

Even in happy homes where parents are in a committed loving relationship and one is absent for extended periods of time, the children suffer emotionally. They can become fearful, angry, and resent the absent parent. In a child's mind the parent's continual absence signals they are not a priority and therefore unloved. If this occurs in stable homes, think of the damage this causes children of divorce.

I have heard countless stories and have read many articles that corroborate this sentiment. Divorce has a massive impact on our children. As parents we must minimize our children's trauma by coping with our own feelings and facilitating the relationship between our children and the other parent. If there are situations where this would be dangerous because of abuse, drug or alcohol problems, or some other extenuating circumstance, as a parent you must protect your children. In these situations, pursuing legal avenues is the top priority.

When tensions are high parents may use their children as messengers. While this seems like an effective way to avoid conflict, it is a terrible decision as it heightens the tension for the children.

Children should never be pawns and placed in that unfair and highly pressured position. They become aware of private information that should only be discussed between adults. It drives them to choose sides. Divorce is an adult issue and when children are brought in this way, the marriage deconstruction becomes their problem. If parents find communication in person is ineffective because of emotional outbursts or lingering anger, it's best to use email. If email doesn't work, outside avenues should be explored such as counseling, mediation, or parenting coordinators.

Additionally, never try and communicate something new to the other parent during pick up and drop off. That is the time to reassure our children of our love for them. Be pleasant and hospitable to the other parent, despite their actions or words. Our children are watching everything, although they may not understand now, as they mature, they will see our good efforts at keeping the peace with the other parent and will be grateful. They will also discern, over time, which parent does this and which one doesn't.

Discipline

When we're overwhelmed it may seem easier to relent and disregard standard discipline. Additionally, divorced parents carry the burden of guilt due to the breakup. This overwhelming guilt causes parents to pity their children and let family rules slide.

This causes children to become self-absorbed and think the world must cater to them. Parents who overindulge their children instill the feeling they can do no wrong and should be exempt from the consequences of their actions. Children readily manipulate these situations in their favor. We have a responsibility to them and to God to discipline them as needed.

Children *need* boundaries and structure. In their world where everything is changing, parents must provide stability. There is a fine line between children expressing their emotions or being outright disrespectful. If adults find it difficult to express their feelings and to understand their own motivations, how much more is this true for children? At times when they're angry about a situation, they may say harsh things to you or about you. It's important to look deeper than their words. Understand the heart of your child. Help them through the emotions they are facing. Love them unconditionally and be consistent.

Our words and actions wield the power to grant security or insecurity. Our words are the mirror by which our children see themselves. We must monitor our tone and model respectful communication. When we correct and discipline without personal attacks, we can discuss their behavior and its effects on themselves and others without criticism. Our children must know they can come to us with their victories, failures, insecurities, and questions, and that we can be trusted.

Discipline builds trust. Consistent discipline deepens the trust our children place in us, because we say what we mean and mean what we say. Clear rules with both rewards and punishment demonstrates commitment and caring to our children.

So, what is appropriate information?

When your child asks, "Why did you and daddy get divorced?" How do you respond? This very delicate question deserves an answer. If there has been adultery, abuse, chemical or sexual addiction, the answer must be appropriate to the age of the child. Some information is simply private.

Getting your children to be on "your side" by disclosing damaging information should never be the agenda. The end goal should be to provide a sense of safety without turning them against marriage itself. Instead, our objective should be to help them understand that marriage is a gift from God, something he planned to be incredibly good.

Corrie Ten Boom provided an excellent example in her book *The Hiding Place*. As a child she read the word "sex sin" and asked what it meant. No one would answer. They stifled her questions, uncertain how to address it. This further flamed her interest in finding out the meaning.

One day she took a train ride with her father. Without the rest of her family around, she asked him. Her father said nothing. For the entire train ride, he appeared to have ignored her question. It seemed she would never get her answer. At their train stop he asked her to carry a big suitcase out of the train. She dutifully agreed.

When she picked it up, she could barely drag it. The weight of it was too much for her small frame.

Her father said, "Corrie, if I made you carry this all the way off the train, I wouldn't be a very good father to you, would I?"

She agreed.

Then he said, "That's the way it is with certain information. It's too heavy for someone so young to carry. Let me carry it for you for now and when you are older, you will be able to carry it for yourself."

We can adopt this position on certain information that would hurt our children. Some are too young to understand the factors that led to your divorce. Even those children old enough to understand don't need to know every detail. Make it a point to be truthful, but sensible in the facts you share with your children.

Maintaining your dignity

Some marriages end amicably. The parties leave because they no longer love each other and have agreed that a divorce is the best option. But let's face it, that's not the norm. It wasn't for me.

Because of the intense wounds that occurred over the years together, it may be difficult to maintain your composure when interacting with your former spouse. During times where you feel the pain again or a strong reaction to it, use extreme self-awareness and practice self-control. Always remember your children are watching and your behaviors affect them. This must be done in spite of the other parent and in spite of the anger and pain.

Below are some guidelines for interactions with your former spouse:

- In situations with high conflict, maintain a business style relationship as it relates to the children. Only convey necessary information—no more and no less. Don't be a "blurter."

- Don't have discussions about money in front of the children.

- Don't argue with your former spouse in front of your children or on the phone.

- Refrain from talking with your children about your former spouse's negative behavior.

- Develop an amicable relationship with your spouse, as soon as possible, and always strive to be polite. This takes time and mental preparation. If you move forward this way, one step at a time you'll eventually get there.

- Choose to focus on and comment on the strengths of each family member.

- Be courteous during pickups and drop offs. This includes arriving on time.

Both research and my personal and professional experience point to the same thing: children who have been exposed to ongoing hostilities between parents retain personal and emotional difficulties that remain into adulthood. The pain doesn't go away and will permeate into their personal relationships.

We have a responsibility to our children to put their needs ahead of our desire to get even. If we alone take the higher road, our behavior is meaningful. Our children will observe our actions, not just our words. By doing the right thing, we let them know how much we love them. Care enough to put your feelings aside for their sake.

Faith

There are wounds only our heavenly Father can heal. This is true not only for you but for your children. For them to walk in wholeness, they must cultivate a relationship with the Lord. We need to teach them that although they have earthly parents, it is their heavenly Father who brings healing, wholeness, love, and peace to their hearts. Our children need to know God as Healer.

"These commandments that I give you today are to be on your hearts. Impress them on your children. Talk about them when you sit at home and when you walk along the road, when you lie down and when you get up. Tie them as symbols on your hands and bind them on your foreheads. Write them on the doorframes of your houses and on your gates" (Deuteronomy 6:6–9).

We need to prioritize conversations with our children about the Lord and his mercies. They should see our love for God as part of our everyday life. It's not enough to send them to church or to say a prayer at dinner or bedtime and think we are imparting Christ into their lives. Worse yet, there are parents who profess to be Christians and appear to in be in right standing before the church congregation, but at home they live below their profession of faith. Half-heartedness is worse than total rebellion. Our desire should be to leave our children a legacy of faith, not hypocrisy.

Teaching children the power of prayer instills in them a deep dependence on God. Prayer should be a part of our everyday life because it is our lifeline to the Lord. Our children need to cultivate their own faith journey. They will experience hardships we can't help them with, but as they learn that they too can trust the Lord, he will help them walk by faith.

The Lord charges us to teach the Word of God to them. Get your children age-appropriate Bibles and read scriptures aloud together as a family. Encourage your children to keep a prayer journal and to learn to thank God for answering prayers for themselves and others. Memorize scripture with them. You can even make a game out of it. This has been an effective way for my family to memorize scripture.

Our prayers on behalf of our children and the biblical principles we teach them will plant deep roots in the soil of their hearts. The Word of God promises us that it will not return empty. If later they rebel or seem far from the Lord, remember God's promise, and the power of his Word and continue to cover them in prayer. A parent's prayer is precious to the heart of God. We have to always hope for the best in them even if they are at their worst. Ask God's wisdom, guidance, power, and protection over their lives.

Exchange discord for calmness by maintaining your dignity.

**TESTIMONY, MONA,
CHILD OF DIVORCED PARENTS**

My home life with my father was tumultuous, even as a young child, I knew something was wrong. When I was seven, my parents divorced, and we moved to a different state. Because I loved my father and my extended family, the separation was devastating.

Through the changes and instabilities, I cannot recall a time my mother spoke negatively about my father. On the contrary, she encouraged us to love him. She went above and beyond to help us maintain a relationship with him. She would call him on our behalf and make us write letters to him. She also kept the relationship with her in-laws, our grandparents, active and open and taught us to love them as well.

Because we lived in another state, we spent time with my father in the summers. This meant travel by plane. As the oldest of three, I felt responsible for my younger siblings. As a parent today, I know how difficult it must have been for my mother to let us go.

Summers with my dad were fun and adventurous. He allowed us to do things my mother would not. We went clubbing, drank, had beach parties . . . a teenager's dream. After a few summers of this, I chose this lifestyle. By this time my mother was happily remarried.

So, full of confidence, while on vacation with my dad, I devastated her with a terrible letter requesting to stay with him for the following school year. I believed this was a reasonable request. I had lived with her for six years and I was only asking for one year with my dad.

She said no. Reluctant and upset, I returned home. What I, at thirteen, thought was her most selfish act, turned out to be the best thing for me. My only regret is causing her so much pain with that letter.

I had a tough time accepting my stepfather, partly because my father "all of a sudden" asked my mom to take him back. She wisely said no, but with my immature thinking, I was angry. Despite my resentment toward her and my stepfather, they continued to love me. Even then, she did not turn me against my father, and I continued my summers with him. In time, I learned to love my stepfather, a good man who loved my mom and treated her the way she deserved.

I have nothing but admiration for my mother, for her example to me in so many ways. I'm grateful she taught me to honor my father, even when he didn't deserve it, and always put our wellbeing before her fears and feelings. As an adult, I realize she cried many private tears and held us up with many silent prayers. Her sacrificial love inspires me.

My parents' divorce impacted me profoundly. As a child of divorce, I know the obstacles children must climb. Their road is difficult, uncertain, and scary. Children need both parents to love them unconditionally and to make a terrible situation better for them. Never tire of doing good. In the future they will honor and love you for it.

"Whatever a man sows, he will reap in return. The one who sows to please his flesh, from the flesh will reap destruction; but the one who sows to please the Spirit, from the Spirit will reap

eternal life. Let us not grow weary in well doing, for in due time we will reap a harvest, if we do not give up" (Galatians 6:7–9).

Children don't get a say when marriages end, but they too suffer the aftermath. Taking a godly position regarding a former spouse instills a sense of stability and guides them in making hard but good choices. Wise decisions will show your children that your character is no longer marred by the stigma of divorce. Just like we lay aside the letter D and embrace Christ as our new identity, our children should replace their label of child of divorce to Child of God.

Christ gives us a new name:
CHILD OF GOD.

CHAPTER TEN: CHILDREN

Prayer

Lord, I want to pass on a legacy of righteousness to my children. Forgive me for the times I have let you down in this area. I know my children are a gift from you and you have given me the responsibility to teach them in your ways (Psalm 127:3; Deuteronomy 11:19). Enable me to model godly character, even when I am angry, frustrated, or sad. Remove hypocrisy from me. I pray my children will see true Christian character and may it encourage them to live a life holy and blameless unto you. Help me to discipline when necessary. May I never provoke my children to wrath, but instead bring them up in the training and admonition of the Lord (Proverbs 13:24).

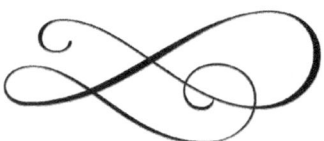

Children are a heritage from the Lord, offspring a reward from him. Like arrows in the hands of a warrior are children born in one's youth. Blessed is the man whose quiver is full of them. They will not be put to shame when they contend with their opponents in court.

—Psalm 127:3–5

Reflection

Before answering these questions, ask the Holy Spirit to bring to mind the areas of your life addressed in this chapter which need healing and change.

1. How are your children coping with the separation of the family unit? Have you provided a safe space for them to talk about the changes in your family? What else can you do to help them speak openly about their feelings?

2. Do your children feel they have to protect you or the other parent because derogatory comments have been made by you, the other parent, or members of your family?

3. Have your children been exposed to your marital conflict? Are they placed in a position where they must choose sides? If yes, what steps will you take in order to avoid this in the future?

4. How much do your children know about the reason(s) for the divorce? Is it appropriate?

5. Do you find it difficult to discipline or set boundaries with your children because of emotional exhaustion or feelings of guilt? If yes, how can that be alleviated?

6. Do you regularly spend time in prayer with them and teach them the Word of God? What steps can you take to implement this on a regular basis?

ELEVEN

Legal Issues

I am not an attorney and am not offering legal or financial advice. If you need legal advice, contact a licensed attorney in your jurisdiction.

When we marry, we enter the union as a covenant, lovingly making vows with every intention of spending a lifetime together. This takes little time; the marriage license is the only document filed with the county. In comparison, divorce is lengthy and arduous. While tortured emotions rage during a divorce, the courts treat the process as a business transaction. Judges expect parties to be polite, poised, and prepared to work through the decisions of the proceedings.

For many, this is impossible. Instead of the courtroom being a place where the details are finalized, it becomes an arena for vindication. Litigation provides the stage where the drama of who will win plays out, usually to the financial and emotional detriment of the whole family.

Each spouse mistakenly believes that, when the facts are presented, the judge will undoubtedly see the truth and implement justice in their favor. Instead, a party's "day in court" frequently produces unexpected results and comes with a devastating emotional and financial price tag.

Judges have busy schedules and frequently lack the time to read through pages and pages of nasty texts and ugly email messages. They have little desire to dig into the fractured and angry details of every case, and despite our ideal of impartial justice, judges do hold preconceived notions. All too often, a battle in the courtroom results in further disappointment and unmet expectations.

Television advertisements portray attorneys as superheroes, fighting tirelessly for a just outcome. Avoid mistaking your attorney for a friend, therapist, or solution to your problems. The attorney's role is to advise clients on the business of divorce, provide strategies on how to proceed, and take the case to court if necessary. It's also important to keep in mind, zealous advocacy comes at a steep hourly rate.

Consulting a lawyer with the expectation of victory is usually a prelude to failure. Such crusades escalate the emotional toll of divorce. Frustration mounts while time and money bleed away. Those who survive lengthy, litigious divorces admit they spent too much time, paid far too much money, and were none the better for it.

To avoid this trap when facing a divorce, consider and discuss alternative approaches to resolving the issues. First, discard the mindset of winning. Then, research and weigh your options to make an informed decision that is best for you and your family. Consider these factors:

- Can I proceed without an attorney? This is called self-help or *pro se*. Depending on your income, many courts have free or low-cost assistance programs for filling out the forms. If the spouses can agree on most of the issues, this can be the easiest, most cost effective, way to go.

- Can mediation resolve the issues? Mediation is proven to work in most cases. As a result, almost all states now require parties to attend mediation prior to fighting it out in court. In mediation, a neutral third party helps the husband and wife negotiate the terms of the divorce, including custody issues, parenting plans, marital settlement agreements, division of assets and liabilities, alimony, child support, and other issues.

  Tax professionals, financial planners, appraisers and/or other professionals can be consulted, as needed, to ensure all the information is correct and up to date for negotiations. The parties do not have to get along for this process to work. They do have to be open to considering options and compromising. Each retains his or her attorney for representation throughout the mediation process or an attorney can be retained to review the final agreement. After this, unresolved issues can be litigated.

- Is collaborative divorce a better choice? In a collaborative approach, each party retains an attorney, agreeing from the outset, in writing, there will be no litigation. A series of group meetings are used to work out the details of the divorce. Typically, neutral financial and mental health professionals attend the meetings and play vital roles in this process.

- Would separate attorneys and litigation work best? This is the most costly and contentious choice because it creates a "you versus them" situation. You become adversaries working against each other. This often creates a self-preservation mode where one attempts to protect themselves from their former spouse at all costs.

Following the divorce, many people wind up back in court over parenting disputes, child-support, alimony, and other financial issues. Solutions such as mediation and collaborative divorce allow parties to sit down together and carefully craft agreements that are less likely to result in litigation after the divorce is over. A person who is forced to comply with a judge's ruling is more likely to go back to court over every disagreement, often with the misguided perception the judge will make the right decision if he or she hears what has happened since the judgment was entered. Think carefully about how you approach your case and whether the resolution is likely to land you back in court in a year or two. Assess and evaluate all the options. Is there a better way to achieve peace and finality?

"Do not bring hastily to court, for what will you do in the end if your neighbor puts you to shame" (Proverbs 25:8).

Co-Parenting/Time-Sharing/Custody

The days of a mother automatically having primary or full custody are no longer the norm. More states now use a timesharing concept which means, in most cases, there is no longer a primary custodial parent who wins.

The goal of timesharing is for the children to spend substantial time with both parents. For this to succeed, parents must work together. The best-case scenario is a co-parenting relationship where reasonable communication results in fair and flexible scheduling and decision-making. Parents adjust to accommodate the needs of the children, as well as the needs and obligations of the other parent. For most families, everyone benefits from this type of cooperative co-parenting relationship.

When parents remain angry and continue to fight, co-parenting is impossible and parallel parenting becomes a better choice. In this model, the parents want a continued relationship with the children, but recognize contact with each other inevitably results in conflict, so they establish strict schedules with little to no flexibility. Any need for a schedule change must be addressed via email to avoid emotional interactions with each other. This keeps the communication in a business-like tone and prevents placing children in the middle of a battle. It also provides a paper trail should a return to court become necessary.

Parallel parenting works well in the beginning when emotions are running high thereby maintaining the children's access to both parents. While this system reduces parental disruption, it's a less desirable choice. Co-parenting is the best option, because it allows the children to integrate all parts of their life and assures them their parents are still working together.

Sometimes a parent recognizes that fighting in front of the children hurts them and rationalizes that it would be better to stop seeing their kids. This detachment adds a burden of loss. Not only do the children have to cope with the separation of their parents, but also with the loss of a parent's presence and participation, and children often blame themselves for it.

When facing divorce, my training as a clinical social worker and professional mediator failed to prepare me for the experience. I sometimes reacted inappropriately and made mistakes. There were instances where I talked about money or argued with their father in the children's presence. He, on the other hand would belittle me in front of them, adding to the conflict. We had to adopt a parallel parenting approach at the beginning of our separation because of painful emotions.

We knew this was wrong, and neither of us wanted to hurt our children. Knowing I couldn't change him, I decided to change myself. Many times, I swallowed my pride and stayed silent, even when I felt he was inappropriate. I disengaged emotionally, ignored his junk behavior, and only responded to important issues.

Time now has passed. Most of our wounds healed and we have developed a better co-parenting relationship. We email each other regarding sensitive issues but are comfortable enough to discuss simple schedule changes. On this bumpy road, we, like many others, have committed to work together for the sake of our children.

It is critical that parents keep their children's needs in mind whenever interacting with the other parent. Our behavior is a testament of love to our children. Are we willing to sacrifice our egos to help them transition? Yes, it is difficult, but maintaining our integrity and treating the other parent with respect, even when they don't deserve it, is one of the best things we can do on behalf of our children.

Exchange contention for peace.

TESTIMONY: ANGELA,
DIVORCED AFTER TEN YEARS OF MARRIAGE

I grew up in the church. As a pastor's daughter there isn't a sermon I haven't heard or a verse I wasn't forced to recite.

My family never had an overflow of money, so I worked hard to avoid that for myself. I attained two master's degrees. For over ten years I was the breadwinner in my marriage. We lived well and I made sure of it.

Then the bottom fell out . . . From one moment to the next I found myself with no electricity, no water, no cable, and a negative bank account. I was now a single mother with two kids in an arduous court battle.

My former husband, a charming and attractive man, became obsessed with my destruction. Throughout our marriage I was clueless about his secret, homosexual life. He began scheming and plotting the divorce for months before acting on it. On more than one occasion, he reached out to friends, family and even our neighbors and claimed I participated in several adulterous relationships.

He spread vicious lies about me, and because he was so convincing, many believed him. Once he felt his story was strong enough, he filed for divorce. Because he gained the pity vote, he was able to borrow money from his family and used the court system as a stage for his vengeance.

I was left with nothing. My legal debts forced me to file for bankruptcy.

When I had no utilities, no place to go, and no one to turn to, I spent the entire night crying out to Jesus. He heard me. It was humbling to admit that I didn't have enough to pay bills, but I heard the still small voice of God tell me "Give me the first." So, I went to the payroll department at my job and gave them my church account number so I could give tithes before I even saw the money. Miraculously, the very next paycheck, I received an increase.

Then I felt the Lord stirring my heart to give an additional 5% of my salary as offerings. I again went to my payroll accountant and had them take out an additional 5%. I struggled with this decision and even thought about reneging on it. But I didn't.

Although I have not always had money for what I want, I have money for everything I need. When I no longer struggled with the decision of tithes and offerings, I felt like I graduated from a spiritual battle.

Several years have passed and my bankruptcy has been resolved. Finances have stabilized, and I have been able to provide my children a beautiful home and security. Thanks be to God for his faithfulness.

Additionally, the truth of my former husband's secret life surfaced. Many who turned their backs on me have since apologized and we have reconciled. God alone has been my vindicator.

Divorce options vary. When spouses agree to make the battle as civil as possible, less time and money are spent, the pain is minimized and children have a smoother transition between homes. But sometimes contentious battles overtake the process. As a Christian, the important choice is to seek God's wisdom and be the one who exemplifies the Lord's character. In time, God can reverse and restore the slander and destruction of others. And, in that, he is glorified in our lives.

Christ gives us a new name:
VIRTUOUS.

CHAPTER ELEVEN: LEGAL ISSUES

Prayer

Lord, I look to you for wisdom and counsel. Guide me through this process and show me who to go to when I need specific knowledge about what to do. Lord, I want to wake up in the morning thinking of you, not the problems that surround me. I know you are in charge of my life and order each one of my steps (Psalm 119:130–136). Help me to keep that in forefront of my mind so I am not filled with dread or anxiety over the future. Overwhelm me with your joy because it is my strength (Nehemiah 8:10). I need your joy today and forever. I thank you because I know your hand is upon me and my family at this time and I choose to believe you will work all things, even this, for your good (Romans 8:28).

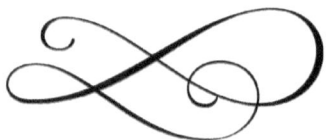

Lord, how many are my foes! How many rise up against me! Many are saying of me, "God will not deliver him." But you, Lord, are a shield around me, my glory, the One who lifts my head high. I call out to the Lord, and he answers me from his holy mountain. I lie down and sleep; I wake again, because the Lord sustains me. I will not fear though tens of thousands assail me on every side. Arise, Lord! Deliver me, my God! Strike all my enemies on the jaw; break the teeth of the wicked. From the Lord comes deliverance. May your blessing be on your people."

—Psalm 3:1–8

Reflection

Before answering these questions, ask the Holy Spirit to bring to mind the areas of your life addressed in this chapter which need healing and change.

1. Have you viewed your divorce as an opportunity for a "win?" If yes, how has this affected you?

2. Have you and your spouse explored cooperative or collaborative options for facilitating a less contentious divorce?

3. If you have children, are you doing your best to cooperate on parenting issues? Is your parenting relationship working for everyone? What are some of the positives and what are some things that can be improved?

TWELVE

When People Ask

People in your life will fall into two categories. Some will offer boatloads of support and compassion, before, during, and after your divorce. Others will not. Some supporters may have less interest in the Bible, while others will be extremely committed to following its directives. Be prepared for unsupportive people who dig up scriptures and quote them with condemnation, questioning how and why you came to this decision.

Who will you trust? How much will you reveal about your personal life? What will you say about the indiscretions and abusive behavior that culminated in the decision to part with your spouse? You can resist the urge to justify yourself to those who voice their disapproval or silently judge you by not throwing your partner to the lions of public opinion.

A Pattern to Follow

Reverse the situation. How would you want to be treated? How much information would you want dispersed among friends and on social media if *you* had been the one to disengage, acting in ways that ended the marriage? Even people who succumb to temptation and make bad decisions dislike being wounded. Unfortunately, we inflict more pain on ourselves when we constantly air private details demonstrating our condemnation rather than forgiveness. Yet the Bible declares, "Love covers a multitude of sins" (I Peter 4:8).

The behavior Jesus modeled throughout his life, the way he died, and the overall character of God displayed from the beginning to the end of the Bible, display the grace and mercy granted to us when *we* deserved condemnation.

The tightrope of divorce dangles us over the chasm of difficult choices while we try to put our lives back together. We can balance ourselves during the challenging walk by focusing on Jesus and the mercy he has poured on our lives.

Consider the example of Jesus on the cross. He didn't slay his persecutors. He didn't curse them. He didn't parade their unspeakable acts of torture before the crowd and promise them hell in eternity. He said, "Father, forgive them for they do not know what they are doing" (Luke 23:34).

But *he's* Jesus.

And *we* have his spirit residing in us, enabling us to respond in the same way. We often view our pain through tunnel vision expecting to walk in God's forgiveness for *our* offenses and yet imprison others for theirs.

We are called to gain God's wisdom from the Bible, live in the power of his Holy Spirit, and reflect him in our public and private lives. "And whatever you do, whether in word or deed, do it all in the name of the Lord Jesus, giving thanks to God the Father through him" (Colossians 3:17). We *can* be a testimony to a world that desperately needs to understand how to live through brokenness and become whole again.

How We Do It

Answers begin with listening. Remember the proverb, "A gentle answer turns away wrath" (Proverbs 15:1).

At some point you'll be questioned or criticized. Before you respond let Jesus lead you. Ask yourself, "what would God have me do?" Recall the Father's instructions on the Mount of Transfiguration when Peter wanted to start building structures for Jesus, Moses, and Elijah. He said, "This is my Son, whom I love; with him I am well pleased. Listen to him" (Matthew 17:5b).

Jesus reinforced this at the Last Supper when he comforted the disciples. "When he, the Spirit of truth, comes, he will guide you into all truth" (John 16:13). Read the Bible often. Daily. Let God's words shape your thoughts. The more you implant them in your heart and mind, the more the Lord will bring them to your memory at just the right time. Compile a list of verses God has used to assure your heart. Reread and share them. Find trusted friends, your own board of directors, to share your more private thoughts and struggles with.

When someone wants to talk to you, be willing to listen, particularly when the person clearly wants to encourage or help. If the circumstances aren't appropriate, schedule a better time. Rather than strategizing verbal comebacks, concentrate on the message while internally offering everything in the conversation to God. Follow these three guidelines. "Everyone should be quick to listen, slow to speak and slow to become angry" (James 1:19).

You may be challenged part way through the conversation, "Well, what do you have to say about that?"

Simply answer, "I'm still listening." This assures the other person that you are paying attention. This excludes abusive comments. In that case, excuse yourself and as calmly as possible, walk away. When the person appears to finish, ask, "Is there anything else?"

While the person gives his or her opinion, bolstered by scripture, ask God to help you understand any truth in the words you hear. Even our best desires to encourage may contain tainted comments and motives. Resist the urge to become defensive or angry. You may hear the words from people, but in the end, you will answer to God for your response. "Always be prepared to give an answer to everyone who asks you to give the reason or the hope that you have. But do this with gentleness and respect, keeping a clear conscience, so that those who speak maliciously against your good behavior in Christ may be ashamed of their slander" (I Peter 3:15–16).

Be careful with your responses—be slow to speak and thoughtful, not rash and reactive. Craft your words as though Jesus himself were speaking softly into your ear, telling you how he wants you to respond and what he wants the other person to hear and learn. The answer God wants you to give may not be to defend yourself but may be designed to benefit the other person. Be discerning and recognize that in any situation, despite your insecurities, unexpressed agendas may exist.

Try to separate the real message from any critical words or attitudes that may have obscured helpful insights. Much of communication is non-verbal. Pay attention to the subtleties of body language and inflection. Take what you know about the character of the speaker and overlay the words with that. It will help you hear what the Lord wants you to hear.

Preparation: Silence and Solitude

When we fall in love, we find ways to spend more time with our beloved. We repeat their words, we glow at the mention of their name, and we pass up other activities to be with them.

Fall in love with Jesus—your most important relationship—the same way. Get quiet so you can listen for that still, small voice. Find a way to have time alone just for him. There will always be distractions, escapes from the pain—TV, our phones, friends, activities, even sleep. Fight the good fight of faith and make time to be with the Lord. Even though children, jobs, and ongoing commitments make it hard; love always finds a way.

So, here's the challenge. Let the one who loves you best, Jesus, know that you want to love him best. You may not find large chunks of time but bypass other options for him. He bypassed the glory of heaven and perfection there to come here and rescue you.

Run to him. Record the thoughts and hopes he gives you. Allow his love to pour over you and wipe your tears. You will gain strength and as your thoughts clear, you will see a path forward.

Words of Peace

Jesus didn't rebut every accusation; He often asked questions to answer questions. He was the perfect listener and in perfect control of his responses. "If it is possible, as far as it depends on you, live at peace with everyone" (Romans 12:18).

You'll be able to be at peace with some, but not all. Some will be loyal and loving. Others, because of their own wounds, will depart, often after saying hurtful things. Remember to love your enemies.

Silence beats eating hasty words. When you daily fill your mind and heart with scripture, you'll recognize the Lord's voice more easily, often providing answers you know *you* didn't devise. The goal isn't to win the argument, but to become more like Jesus. Whatever others say or write to you as advice should align with the Bible; that's always the test. Be sure to stay focused on God's Word.

Practice using these answers:

- I understand.
- I appreciate your interest and concern.
- I've prayed and will consider your input.
- I've searched the scripture and sought God.
- I've consulted wise Christians for advice.
- I realize we may not agree on this, but I still care that you want to help me.
- I understand that my relationship with the Lord is about his grace and mercy despite my failings. My identity is safe in him because of what he did for me.
- I'm still learning that I'm truly weak, but God is strong.
- Thank you.

Exchange justification with wisdom.

TESTIMONY: AMANDA,
SINGLE AFTER THREE FAILED MARRIAGES

When I was nineteen, I delivered a full-term, stillborn baby girl. My husband and I had stayed with my parents the last part of my pregnancy while he completed an internship, so we were across the state from the college we attended. In 1970, there were no support groups for women who lost babies at birth. There was no discussion and little comfort offered. Family, friends, even my doctor said, "Go back to college and get on with your life." As if her death was unimportant.

I can't count the number of times I also heard, "You'll have other children." I learned never to say that to anyone.

Two months later my husband started seeing his former girlfriend and moved out. She came to visit him from out of state and he thought it would be a good idea to stop by with her and introduce us. A good idea? He wanted a divorce so he could get on with his life.

There were no divorce recovery groups either.

I'd gone to church with my family my whole life until college. For years I'd been exposed to the Bible but had no personal connection to Jesus. After my divorce, I decided to go to a church with the hope I'd find help there. The nearby, well-attended Baptist church had a revival going on. I sat near the front. When the speaker talked about sin, I considered the wreckage of my life after a mere two decades of living and agreed I was a sinner. Then he said emphatically and repeated two or three times, "Divorce is a sin. If you get a divorce for any reason, you can never remarry and be in God's will."

He went on to talk about Jesus and salvation, but I heard little after that definitive, disturbing pronouncement. Waves of despair crashed around me, blocking out any light from the message about salvation. Wanting no part of the kind of God the speaker presented to me, I actually gripped the back of the pew in front of me to avoid doing the walk down the aisle.

For the next couple of years, which I remember little of, I chose a path of personal destruction. Then in the summer of 1972, a friend from my hometown shared the gospel and took me to an out-of-town weekend event where I quit running from God.

I returned to college, saved, but without a single Christian friend. After several weeks of visiting churches, I discovered I had a Christian classmate. She took me to church and introduced me to a young man who was passionate about his faith. He got me involved in an off-campus Bible study and we married shortly after that. The group turned out to be a cult.

Six weeks into the marriage, he started cheating on me, always followed by demands that I must forgive him and have sex with him, or I wasn't a good Christian. Then he relapsed into drug use. I kept all of this secret. When we did go to a traditional church, people shied away rather than trying to talk to us about our off-site Bible study. They acted as though we'd chosen to follow the devil and walked away from us, whispering, and looking pointedly at us from across the fellowship hall. No one offered any counsel or help.

Months later the teachings of the cult and the isolation they demanded came to a head. Hours of searching the scriptures led to a conversation where we said we could no longer accept their theology. So, they walked us out the door and said that no one from the group would talk to us again. We had no one but each other, and he was no consolation.

Meanwhile my husband's bizarre and abusive behavior grew worse. Three years into our marriage I quit counting the jobs he got and quit or got and was fired from. I stopped at forty-two. Then we became part of a Jesus house ministry.

I was crumbling under the pressure of pretending I was okay around these Christians but felt no one was safe enough to confide in about my home situation. No one understood the nightmare I was living. I prayed every night he wouldn't come home and in a drug-and-alcohol clouded state and kill me in my sleep. I still suffer from insomnia because of this trauma.

When my husband abruptly broke off our connection to the house church, I left him and sought refuge with my mother. She took me to a counselor who, among other things, urged me not to listen to his pleadings and return to a dangerous situation. Feeling like I couldn't fail at marriage again, I returned.

One friend from the house ministry told me that the others felt I deserved to have my marriage fall apart because we had left the group. They didn't know I had no voice in that decision. Once again, I found that Christians were better at stabbing the wounded than healing them.

Things got worse. I nearly died from a misdiagnosed ectopic pregnancy, because although I was hemorrhaging, my husband didn't want to consult my doctor. He had worked that day and was tired. A friend shamed him into calling the doctor who sent us to the hospital. Failure number two with both marriage and pregnancy.

I heard a shift in teaching when I tried another church. Depending on the appropriate designation of fault, some Christians would agree that since I wasn't born again when my first husband left, it was possible that God would accept this second marriage. But I must be sure to make this one work because now I was a Christian and that meant any marital failure would bar me from another marriage.

At the end of five and a half miserable years, on the verge of suicide, I left him. It turned out his female friend from work who I had cooked dinner for shortly before our divorce became his next wife a couple of months later.

My third marriage lasted longer because I was too stubborn to give up, even when after ten years, he'd changed careers and for the next ten years separated himself from almost any contact with me or the few friends we shared. We had no children and coexisted more like roommates while I worked two jobs to pay the bills. When certain choices he'd made came to light, there was no turning back. He had no interest in repairing our relationship or going to counseling, so I got to chalk up my third failure.

People don't always say it, but everyone has heard unspoken comments. What in the world is wrong that you failed not once, but three times? You must really be a mess!

A certain grace surrounds those who survive one mistake and make the next work. Not so much for those who have a series of failures. This club is not one any sane person wants to join, especially not a Christian. So those of us in membership must learn to offer others the kindness and grace that has so frequently been withheld from us. That is following Jesus.

People will fall into one of two categories during and after divorce. Some will bring baskets of condemnation while patting themselves on the back for having a good marriage. They often have scripture to share that twists the knife of pain even deeper. Others bring a basket of listening compassion and offer scriptures to help with healing. In both cases, having kind and gentle responses pleases the Lord and illuminates the C of identity in Christ.

Christ gives us a new name:
GODLY.

CHAPTER TWELVE: WHEN PEOPLE ASK

Prayer

Lord, I want to revere your ways and seek your truth. I want to be a person who is quick to listen and slow to speak. May I reflect your character, even when I am misjudged. Do not let bitterness or resentment take residence in me from others insensitivity. Help me to not be defensive but instead to glean wisdom and insight from the words of others. I want to hear your counsel above all others (Proverbs 19:21). May I keep my eyes on you as you are the Author and Finisher of my faith (Hebrews 12:2). You are still writing my story and because you love me, you will keep me in perfect peace as I keep my eyes on you (Isaiah 26:3).

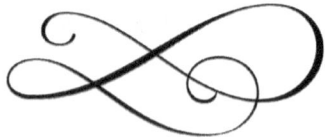

"I lift up my eyes to the mountains— where does my help come from? My help comes from the Lord, the Maker of heaven and earth. He will not let your foot slip— he who watches over you will not slumber; indeed, he who watches over Israel will neither slumber nor sleep. The Lord watches over you— the Lord is your shade at your right hand; the sun will not harm you by day, nor the moon by night. The Lord will keep you from all harm— he will watch over your life; the Lord will watch over your coming and going both now and forevermore."

—Psalm 121

Reflection

Before answering these questions, ask the Holy Spirit to bring to mind the areas of your life addressed in this chapter which need healing and change.

1. In what situations do you feel as though you have to justify yourself and the decision to divorce? How has this impacted your relationships?

2. Based on the advice from this chapter, what strategies will you implement the next time you feel defensive?

3. Have I given my heart to Jesus and am I spending more time reading the Bible to better understand the heart of God?

Love Again?

The desire to be in a committed loving relationship is a godly one. God created us to be in relationship, for some that companionship comes through marriage. If this is your desire, God will honor it, in his time.

I give my life to you, O Forever Love
For you have shown me the purest of love.
As you take my hand, security comes through.
When others reject me because I'm unlovely,
I look in your eyes and see a reflection of beauty.
As you lift me up in your embrace, a smile shines on my face.
As we dance the night away, joy fills this once empty place.
O Forever Love may it always be like this,
As I bask in your exquisite light for all eternity.

However, before this can take place we should go through a process of healing and wholeness. Before dating, consider the following:

- What indicators of healing signal I'm ready to date again?

- What am I looking for in a relationship?

- Am I looking for someone to complete or complement me?

- In what ways do I focus on the past? The present?

- When do I struggle with sadness over my divorce?

- How did I contribute to the demise of my marriage and how can I avoid those things in the future?

Am I Ready?

I have trusted God with many areas of my life. I've had faith for many things, but when it came down to it, I didn't trust him with my love story. Disillusionment and disappointment caused me to think God didn't care if I had a companion.

For years I spent so much of my life yearning for a love that would complete me. One that would heal those areas of my life devastated by rejection and insecurities. Someone to love me just as I am; one who felt like home.

Divorce forced me to understand I will never find completion in the arms of another. Putting that type of expectation on a relationship is unrealistic and destructive. Others cannot accomplish what only God can do. We are only complete in Christ.

This truth changed my perspective and caused me to wait on God and his timing instead of trying to rush into another relationship. I wanted to wait for the one he had for me.

Rejection

"It is me they are rejecting not you. They don't want me to be their king any longer" (1 Samuel 8:7b).

These are the heartbreaking words spoken by God when his special possession (Israel) rejected him and insisted on an earthly king. They foolishly traded God's glory for the exalted position of a man.

After a divorce, when our hearts are broken and vulnerable, instead of abiding in the presence of God and seeking comfort from him, many fantasize about being romanced in the arms of a man. It's easy to get caught up in the attention and admiration. But how many compromises are made along the way? How many times have we traded the glory of God for the pleasure of a person?

Only God can fully satiate the longing in our hearts. He wants the best for us and as we trust him, in his time and in his way, he will put the correct person in our path. But we must put God first. After not choosing well the first time around, I didn't want to take matters into my own hands and make another mistake. I wanted God's will for my life—fully and completely.

I heard the still small voice that assured me I would marry again. I chose to believe God would redeem my love story.

Old Baggage

The interactions and pain from previous relationships have a way of rearing their ugly head. Things we thought were once resolved sneak up when we least expect it. This was definitely the case for me.

While married, I was constantly berated and criticized. Nothing I did was ever good enough. This caused me to doubt myself and fueled feelings of worthlessness and fear of failure. I was on constant fix mode, making sure everything was in line so there wouldn't be any eruptions. Walking on egg-shells became a way of life.

I was deliberate in assessing and addressing the ways I contributed to the demise of my marriage. Yet, this area remained unresolved. I was scared of not doing things well enough or not measuring up. Whenever something didn't go as planned, I feared backlash or abandonment. This put undue stress on my relationships.

Fear is not of God. It destroys and undermines the good things he gives us. I am a work in progress. So, I thank him for all the times things have not gone as expected and my fears were exposed. Although uncomfortable, each has been a pleasant surprise, teaching me to trust and depend on him.

God continues to mold my character and rebuild the areas of my heart I assumed restored. Peace is replacing anxiety; assurance is erasing fears of inadequacy and failure. I didn't want to take these negative mindsets into my next relationship and damage someone else.

Toads Along the Way

Maintaining our convictions in the dating world is difficult. I made the decision to abstain from sexual intercourse until I was married. I was told countless times how antiquated that is or that no man would ever wait. None of this changed my mind. I wanted to please God and do things right this time around. I knew he would bless my obedience.

It's important to understand, that if a partner is unwilling to wait and honor you by maintaining their purity during the dating process, there's an increased chance they won't be faithful in the challenging times of marriage.

So, I waited over three years before I went on my first date. This person presented so many good qualities. He was a Christian, had a great personality, and we were very compatible. He understood my convictions and embraced them.

Things were great for the first couple of months. Then he vanished. No call. Nothing. That abrupt abandonment with no explanation or warning brought back issues I thought were resolved.

I felt betrayed again. I saw a future with him, so his sudden departure made me feel foolish and undesirable. With no real answers, I examined the red flags of behavior I'd chosen to ignore. Bottom line, he wanted a physical relationship, and when he realized he wasn't going to get one, he moved on.

While premarital sex was my line in the sand, it pointed to others. The issues God brings to your attention may be different. It may be an addiction, subtle abuse, or attempts to dominate and control. Whatever it is that God raises a red flag over—listen to him. Pay attention. The Lord warns us of dysfunction for our good. When he points out a road that will lead us into another pit, he does it so he can redirect us into a good future.

I chose to obey the Lord and it caused me to lose someone I cared about. Not once, but now twice. This became a playground for the enemy of my soul. Thoughts raced through my mind telling me, *"See, you will always be alone." "You're not worth it." "Just give up, it's easier to be like everyone else."* God needed to heal the wounds these lies created.

Not Even Worth a Final Goodbye

A wasteland of broken dreams.
Faithful servant,
Lover of Your heart
On an endless pursuit.
All the striving, all the pain—
Where is the recompense?
All around others rejoice.
Living the dream I hoped would be mine.
Here I stand, alone;
With a pen in hand and my heart in the other.
Weathered and beaten
Used and abused
Working toward my someday
Waiting for my suddenly
Take my hand, I'm so confused.
Tear-stained pillow and tired eyes;
Trying to smile.
Holding on to my faith
Trusting you will pull me through.
The ache I carry—the loneliness inside
The pain is too real—
Abandonment can't lie
Not even worth a final goodbye.
I took a risk and gambled my life
If only I'd seen where this road would end;

Maybe we were better off as friends.
Now it's too late—the wound is too real
Trying to heal,
Praying that God will take it away,
Meanwhile regretting my latest mistake.

So, I was back where I started. I needed to heal once again. I found with lots of prayer and drawing closer to God, the following also helped me through:

- Time with friends and family. In the past I would isolate and not tell anyone about what I was going through. The divorce process taught me how to express my innermost feelings, even when I felt foolish. With this new round of heartbreak, I already had my supports in place. I was able to talk it through with them and they offered the emotional help I needed. I also had time to decompress and laugh. My friends and family offered a shoulder to lean on and good laughs along the way.

- Exercise and lots of it. Physical exertion became a way to dissolve inner pressures and release stress.

- Seek out new experiences and adventures. Rather than staying home and wallowing in self-pity, not wanting to repeat that pattern. I intentionally did things that were fun. I went salsa dancing, rode rollercoasters, played board games, and went indoor skydiving.

- Cry when needed. I learned to not stuff my feelings. Waves of emotions would come at different times. When they did, I cried.

- Pray and read my Bible. In the beginning, most of my prayers were sobs. I cried and cried and then cried more. I talked to God about how I felt. It was a moment-by-moment endeavor. I felt waves of peace flood over me as I spent time in prayer and in God's Word. Meditating on the promises in the Bible remind my anxious heart to wait on him.

Love is Accepted, Not Earned

When a diamond is placed in the correct hands, it is treasured and secure. In the wrong ones, it will be treated casually or discarded. Yet, the value of the diamond is independent from the perception of the one holding it. *You are a diamond.* Perhaps you do not know your worth. Maybe others chose to throw you away. However, the circumstances and things that surround you don't diminish your worth. You are a precious, beautiful child of the Most High God.

One of my favorite love stories in the Bible is found in Genesis 29, when Jacob falls in love with Rachel. From the moment they met, he was smitten, and nothing would stand in his way. He worked in the heat of day herding animals for fourteen years for her hand in marriage.

That blows my mind.

He was so enamored by her that the thought of being with her made it all worthwhile. "And Jacob served seven years for Rachel; and they seemed unto him but a few days, for the love he had to her" (Genesis 29:20, KJV).

After fulfilling his commitment, Rachel's father, Laban, tricked Jacob into marrying her older sister. Despite the deception, he agreed to work another seven years for his beloved.

He valued her. *She was his diamond.* Yet, Rachel didn't see herself that way. She spent the majority of her life fighting for something she already possessed. Focused on what she didn't have, Rachel wasted away trying to earn Jacob's love by giving him children. She agonized and felt inadequate. All the while he loved her.

How many of us do the same? We work to earn a love we already possess. Instead of accepting, we doubt our worthiness to receive it. Walls are erected because of our insecurities. Fear of not measuring up or of being abandoned sabotage the gift placed in our hands.

This applies not only to our earthly relationships, but also to our relationship with God. We work to earn his love and acceptance, and place unrealistic demands on ourselves to measure up. But God isn't looking for perfection. All he wants is our hearts. We can never do enough to earn his love; that's why it's a gift. He lavishes it upon us; all we have to do is receive it.

"No power in the sky above or in the earth below—indeed, nothing in all creation will ever be able to separate us from the love of God that is revealed in Christ Jesus our Lord" (Romans 8:39, NLT).

You are Worth Pursuing

Genesis 1 states that on the sixth day, God created Adam from the dust of the earth. He then gave him the exhaustive task of tending the garden and naming all the animals.

Experiencing the beauty of creation, Adam felt a longing in his heart as he grew to understand in all the earth he did not have a compatible match. Only God could have timed that so perfectly. God allowed Adam to see and experience the entire splendor of creation so he could understand he was missing something, a helper—his companion. God then created Eve from Adam's rib. He blessed man and woman and instructed them to be fruitful and multiply. This has been the Maker's design throughout creation.

I believe it is the same today. It's not until a man realizes there is more to life than work and self-interests, that he is open to pursue and nurture the woman God has created for him. "It is not good that man should be alone; I will make him a helper comparable to him" (Genesis 2:18).

As women, we undermine ourselves by trying to win the love and affection of men who aren't ready to commit. We throw our pearls to the swine and fall too hard and too fast for someone who is not ready for us, thereby putting our hearts in danger (Matthew 7:6).

Men need to know the value God places on a wife. You are worth pursuing.

"He who finds a wife finds a good thing, and obtains favor from the Lord" (Proverbs 18:22).

"Who can find a virtuous wife? For her worth is far above rubies" (Proverbs 31:10).

"A wife of noble character is her husband's crown, but a disgraceful wife is like decay in his bones" (Proverbs 12:4).

Date to Mate

I don't know about you, but I soon realized I didn't want to waste time, energy, or affection on the wrong person. As a result, I adopted a new way to date. I treated it as an interview. There was an open position in my life, and I was considering candidates.

I'm not advocating talking about marriage on the first date—we need to exercise wisdom. However, we should know what we're looking for in a partner and what some of the non-negotiables are. There's no perfect man just as there is no perfect woman, but it's just as important to know and understand what you *don't* want as well as what you *are* looking for.

Meddle

Hurry up and wait . . . We wait in line, we wait for others, we wait for problems to be resolved. We wait . . .

Imagine waiting well into your nineties for one of God's promises to be fulfilled. That would frustrate even the strongest heroes of faith—and it did. God promised Abraham and Sarah a son. They waited . . . and waited . . . and waited.

Nothing.

Then Sarah did what most of us would do. She took matters into her hands. It made sense, and it was the custom of the day. If she couldn't have children, her servant, Hagar, could do it for her. Seemed simple enough (Genesis 16).

It didn't take long for Sarah to regret her decision. But instead of taking responsibility for her part in sinning against God, she unleashed her frustration on Hagar and then blamed Abraham for her decision to go ahead of God's timetable.

I've been tempted to do the same. I know the promises of God for my life, and when they're derailed or slow in coming, I meddle by attempting to work out problems on my own without taking the time to consult God. Most times, it doesn't end well. My impulsive actions have brought dire consequences.

However, as I reflect, each delay has been a stepping-stone used by God to draw me closer to valuable lessons. Perhaps the areas of my life that are on hold are a part of his plan. It's quite likely that God is using the waiting season to mold my character.

God was merciful to both Abraham and Sarah. He fulfilled his promise in a way they never imagined. That encourages me, knowing my expectations don't limit God. He can stretch the boundaries and do the impossible. "The Lord kept his word and did for Sarah what he promised. In her old age she became pregnant and gave birth to a son. *This happened at just the time God said it would*" (Genesis 21:1–2 NLT emphasis added).

There are times in our lives when God opens doors for us, or shuts them, not only for our benefit, but also for the benefit of those we influence. What happens when a plant is uprooted in the heat of summer? It withers and dies. Summer is not the optimal time for transplanting plants. Timing is everything.

God, our master gardener, has a design for the landscape of our lives, but we have to wait for his timing. We could tell him our plans and he could agree with all of them. Yet, if we rush the change and it occurs in the summer of our lives, it will be to our detriment. We must wait for him to determine the right time and the right season.

God reconstructed my broken heart and made it new. In his faithfulness, he brought a wonderful man into my life. My husband came by way of unusual circumstances, when I least expected it. When I remarried, I was able to give him my whole heart, not the fractured pieces of a woman scorned. The heartbreak and lessons of the past have better equipped me for the challenges of remarriage.

It's easy to become discouraged when God's timetable does not line up with our own. Let us continue to pursue wisdom and virtue while trusting the Lord with every step of our life and future.

Exchange insecurity for trust.

TESTIMONY: LIZ NIEVES,
WIDOWED AFTER TWENTY-FIVE YEARS OF MARRIAGE

Cue in the Alfred Hitchcock background music . . . that's how I felt when I decided I was ready to love again. The suspense of what ifs, how, and when could overwhelm anyone. But even in this area of my life, I know I have to completely trust my Lord and Savior Jesus Christ. I had to believe if he had made me whole from loss, if he had healed my heart, he would be with me as I stepped into the daunting world of dating.

It has taken me a while to get here, but I knew my heart was ready. God gave me grace and wisdom to wait on the right timing for my children. When I spoke with them and shared my heart regarding moving on, they responded so lovingly, "Mom, we want you to be happy."

Oddly enough, that wasn't how everyone felt.

"Why not?" I asked. "I'm not Mother Teresa!" This was my response, on more than one occasion, to counter the disbelief from family and friends that I would like to remarry one day.

"Why do you want to do that?" my mother asked.

"Yeah, right," others mockingly replied.

As if making the decision to move on wasn't difficult enough, now I had to justify it?

At that point I realized my future dating and marriage would be completely between God and me. There would be no calls or texts, "Hey, girl, I have the perfect guy for you." This was going to be harder than I thought. So after much prodding from a friend, I decided to try online dating.

That's when my Alfred Hitchcock movie turned into Ripley's Believe It or Not! What I have encountered so far has been almost comical.

"I'm looking for someone stable to have a sexual relationship with." Code: I'm married and want something on the side.

"I can't video chat with you because I'm on a military base and it's for security reasons." Code: I'm not who I say I am.

"I don't know what's wrong with my phone, I can't send selfies." Code: I'm not who I say I am.

"I know I'm younger than you, but I need a mature woman." Code: I'm looking for a cougar.

I can't believe women fall for this!

Now, there have been a couple of men I've had good conversations with, who are sweet and kind. But I just knew they weren't the one. It's hard to explain except that when that still small voice tells me, "Move on," I listen. Too many times we force something because we don't want to be alone. But I refuse to settle. I'd rather be alone than in a mediocre relationship.

I made the decision to abstain from sex until marriage. And that is not always met with enthusiasm, even from "Christian" men. But besides believing that is what God would have me do, I also have seen too many relationships on a road to nowhere because the woman has given all of herself before a true commitment was made. I've also been a witness to relationships that have disintegrated after marrying because sex got in the way of a true courtship. As women, when we give our bodies away, our heart and soul go with it and many times we remain in bad relationships because we've given all we have.

I have to say that at times I have found myself angry with Christian women that have compromised themselves and given themselves so freely that the dating world is forever changed. When it comes to dating in this day and age, I feel I was not born "for such a time as this." Seriously, God, what were you thinking?

But He reminds me: "For my thoughts are not your thoughts, neither are your ways my way" (Isaiah 55:8).

Then I find myself praying for those women that have never been genuinely loved by a man and so they turn a blind eye to red flags, lower their standards, compromise their beliefs in order to be loved. I pray they know their worth, find healing and are able to depend on the Lord Jesus Christ until their husband comes along.

So where does that leave me? Trusting in the Lord. That trust gives me peace. That trust gives me hope. And for now, I'm enjoying "me" time, enjoying my family until the time that I hear those words again, "Babe, what's for dinner?"

Be blessed.

The path to remarriage is different for each person. But God is the one who orchestrates a new beginning, just like he bestows a new identity and new name. We need to trust that while he assures us we are worth being pursued, he will guide each step of our path.

Christ gives us a new name:
PRECIOUS.

CHAPTER THIRTEEN: LOVE AGAIN?

Prayer

Lord, I want to live in the joy and wholeness you have for me. You know my heart's desire and I pray that in your time and in your way, you will meet that. Help me to wait on you and not take matters into my own hands. Give me the perseverance and assurance that you are on the throne and have not forgotten me. I know you care about my love story and there is no greater one than you in my life. Where my heart has been broken in the past, I pray that you would heal it. Increase my faith, that it may not waiver, especially when things don't go as I planned. Help me to make choices that line up with your Word and lead me into the future you have for me.

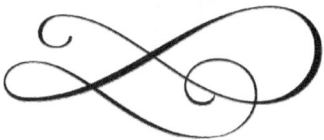

"Blessed are those whose help is the God of Jacob, whose hope is in the Lord their God. He is the Maker of heaven and earth, the sea, and everything in them—he remains faithful forever. He upholds the cause of the oppressed and gives food to the hungry. The Lord sets prisoners free, the Lord gives sight to the blind, the Lord lifts up those who are bowed down, the Lord loves the righteous. The Lord watches over the foreigner and sustains the fatherless and the widow, but he frustrates the ways of the wicked."

—Psalm 146:5–9

Reflection

Before answering these questions, ask the Holy Spirit to bring to mind the areas of your life addressed in this chapter which need healing and change.

1.   What makes me believe I'm ready to start a new relationship?

2.   Describe what this would look like?

3.   Have you lost hope in loving again? Have you been honest with God about this? Ask him to give you a new perspective on your life and future.

FOURTEEN

New Identity

The following Scripture is one I've held close to my heart. I held that pain. I was that young bride abandoned by her husband. There were times I felt abandoned by God; times when everything around me was broken. I felt alone, living in shame and disgrace.

> "Do not be afraid; you will not be put to shame. Do not fear disgrace; you will not be humiliated. You will forget the shame of your youth and remember no more the reproach of your widowhood. For your Maker is your husband— the LORD Almighty is his name—the Holy One of Israel is your Redeemer; he is called the God of all the earth. **The LORD will call you back as if you were a wife deserted and distressed in spirit—a wife who married young, only to be rejected,**" says your God. "For a brief moment I abandoned you, but with deep compassion I will bring you back. In a surge of anger I hid my face from you for a moment, but with everlasting kindness I will have compassion on you," says the LORD your Redeemer" (Isaiah 54: 3b–8, emphasis added).

During this daunting and overwhelming season, I believed the lie I was now used goods. But these verses spoke to me and reminded me that God knew my pain. He understood my grief saturated life. His eye was on me, and he would rebuild my broken ruins. He promised to protect me, to teach my children, and to give us peace. At a time of instability, this promise comforted me. He restored my stability and gave me hope.

I was that storm-battered city, troubled, and desolate. When I looked at my situation through my finite understanding I saw hopelessness, desolation, and despair. When I meditated on the Word of God, I realized that because I had been through a traumatic event there would be a process to heal and rebuild. Everything that lay crumbled at my feet would not be fixed overnight.

There all along
Nothing remained—scattered and worn.
Hopelessly defeated—an open grave
Yet your eye was upon me;
You never gave up.
And now I can see your kindness is true-
Always loving, faithful and pure.
As I look back, you were there all along
You never left, now I sing a new song.
Hallelujah to my Lord, Messiah, and King
The One who redeems.
The One who inspires.
The One who took me out of the mire.
I praise your name.
I am yours forever, a beautiful bride.
Crowned with grace, your blood paid the price.
By my side you will always be;
With your love eternal, and grace upon me.

Instead of leaving me in the ruins, my Creator was fashioning my life into something more beautiful than I could imagine. Because I have a good future to look forward to, I no longer need to identify myself with the "event of divorce." I don't have to let damaging experiences, negative words, or the opinions of others dictate my future.

I can rip off the scarlet letter of reproach and be free to be the person God created me to be.

Life Lessons

Our experiences mold our character. I learned valuable lessons during the difficulties of my previous marriage. When you do something wrong in life you have the choice of either growing from the mistake or repeating it. We can easily get caught up in the cycle of berating ourselves and becoming our own worst critics. Every time we do this we invite unneeded condemnation and live in a cycle of regret and guilt.

God wants us to live in victory. We must forgive ourselves and let go of the baggage of our past mistakes. We cannot rewrite history, but we take the time to examine our shortcomings and grow from them.

We all have struggles. It's tempting to see others and think they have it all together. Their small burdens can pale in comparison to ours. Comparing ourselves to others only brings heartache and pain. We all know only too well the sting the presence of a happy and loving couple brings. Comparison causes us to doubt God's plan for our lives, makes us feel unwanted, and perpetuates a feeling of low self-worth and self-pity.

Throughout the Bible there are many examples of God using the discarded or those who were least valued to accomplish amazing things. Our own Savior came from lowly beginnings. Rumors that he was born out of wedlock followed him into his ministry as a way of discrediting him.

He was criticized and called horrible names. Few expected him to amount to anything. Those who judged with their carnal senses lost the greatest blessing of all time. Scripture records how amazed the Pharisees and Sadducees were by his teaching because they could not believe such wisdom and authority could come from "someone like him."

You may feel this way about yourself. Many divorced people feel they let God down and aren't worthy of his forgiveness. Others feel disenfranchised because they lack emotional and spiritual support. Others leave the church because of these same feelings and unfortunately many churches are ill-equipped to help divorced people.

Looking at the Mirror of God's Word

> "Anyone who listens to the Word but does not do what it says is like someone who looks at his face in a mirror and, after looking at himself, goes away and immediately forgets what he looks like. But whoever looks intently into the perfect law that gives freedom and continues in it—not forgetting what they have heard, but doing it—they will be blessed in what they do" (James 1:23–25).

The Word of God is a mirror. God shows us how to live our lives in order to please him and to receive his blessings. Like real mirrors, we won't always like what we see. There will be scarred and distorted areas of our lives that God wants us to change. The response we have to our reflection determines our dedication to him. Are we willing to submit to God and become the person he wants us to be? Or do we want to keep running our lives, knowing how bad the results have been?

> "Therefore, get rid of all moral filth and the evil that is so prevalent and humbly accept the word planted in you, which can save you. Do not merely listen to the word, and so deceive yourselves. Do what it says" (James 1:21–22).

To produce the righteousness of God we must do the following:

- Lay aside all filthiness by setting aside sin and evil desires. Continual sin in our lives is evidence of a heart rebelling against God.

- Receive with meekness the implanted Word which can save our soul. We must know the Word of God and apply it, even when we don't want to. To apply it, we have to make time to read it for ourselves. God speaks to our hearts through the Bible and the Holy

Spirit provides guidance. God chooses to reveal himself to us by his Word. It is our responsibility to study and meditate on it.

There are times our decisions, selfishness, laziness, impulsiveness, and lack of self-control puts us in the wrong places. This was a hard pill for me to swallow. I was angry over the time I wasted throughout my marriage. I was not where I wanted to be in life. Once I understood God is the Redeemer of my past, present, and future, I was finally able to let go of the "should have been" and live in the "what is going to be."

God can help turn our situations around and make the best use of our time, talents, and resources. We need to take the first step and ask him to help us find the direction to take. Sometimes we remain stuck just waiting for God to tell us what to do. If we obey the words we read in the Bible, the dreams and goals we have will line up with his will. That could mean going back to school, changing careers, writing a book, or even starting a business. Don't sit back waiting around for one day. Make a prayerful plan, act, and if you don't know where to start, ask someone who has already done it. Don't let your insecurities stop you. No one can do it for you, and the Lord will help you every step of the way.

"Commit to the LORD whatever you do, and he will establish your plans" (Proverbs 16:3).

Doubt Transformed

Mark 9:14–29 recounts the journey of a father who searched for a cure for his son's violent seizures. The demon behind this torment often forced the son into fire or water in order to kill him.

This father watched his beloved son suffer for years. I can imagine he tried everything to heal him, living in terror between episodes, and constantly worried that one day he would wake up and find his son dead. The anxiety and the perpetual fear of the unknown must have been overwhelming.

Then he heard about Jesus and of the healing miracles he performed. After exhausting every other resource, this rabbi would be the answer. The father searched, but Jesus was not there—a great disappointment.

When he asked the disciples for help, the situation went from bad to worse. Not only did the disciples not heal the boy, but the spirit manifested in front of an audience. The crowd grew larger and larger, watching the spectacle of the disciples trying to cast this demon out. Arguments and yelling erupted and the whole scene must have made a hurting and disappointed father more distressed and less hopeful.

When Jesus arrived, the crowd left the spectacle and rushed to greet him. The disciples brought the boy to Jesus. Immediately the boy convulsed and fell to the ground writhing and foaming at the mouth. Instead of reacting, Jesus discussed the boy's condition with the father.

During the conversation, a transformation started. The disappointed father began to have a glimmer of hope. He asked Jesus, "have mercy on us and help us, if you can?"

In verses 23 and 24 Jesus responded, "What do you mean, 'If I can?'" Jesus asked. "Anything is possible if a person believes." The father instantly cried out, "I do believe, but help me overcome my unbelief!"

Because of past experiences the father had little expectation for a cure. He came to Christ with a measure of hope but that was dashed by the disciples' failure in Christ's absence. When he saw Christ face to face, his hope was rekindled, but doubt still clouded his mind.

Has disillusionment and disappointment caused you to doubt God's care for you?

Just like the man in this narrative, Christ deals with our letdowns and setbacks one on one. He reminds us that in spite of our past disappointments and failed efforts, he not only wants to help us, but he will. As we draw closer to God, our impatient hearts will learn to wait on the Lord and his time.

I have had a front row seat to God rebuilding the ruins of my life. My experiences have allowed me to understand the devastation of divorce. Because God has graciously healed me, I, in turn, can minister his peace and wholeness to the lives of those going through it. My suffering has not been in vain. God is using it in a beautiful way.

"'For I know the plans I have for you,' declares the LORD, "plans to prosper you and not to harm you, plans to give you hope and a future. Then you will call on me and come and pray to me, and I will listen to you. You will seek me and find me when you seek me with all your heart'" (Jeremiah 29:11–13).

God has a good future and a good hope for you.

Suddenly

The words suddenly and in an instant/instantly appear in Scripture 133 times—each time usurping the status quo.

God is not limited by our logic and reason. Our lives can change in an instant. The prayers we've prayed can be answered in unimaginable ways.

"I waited patiently for the Lord to help me, and he turned to me and heard my cry. He lifted me out of the pit of despair, out of the mud and the mire. He set my feet on solid ground and steadied me as I walked along. He has given me a new song to sing, a hymn of praise to our God. Many will see what he has done and be amazed. They will put their trust in the Lord" (Psalm 40:1–3 NLT).

In our brokenness we gain a deeper understanding of his loving presence, and if we wait on him, he will steady and strengthen us. God can redeem even the ugliest circumstances. He can make something more beautiful out of the splintered pieces of our lives than if they remained intact.

We must be willing to trust and surrender everything to him, even our dreams. He knows what they are and, in his time, and in his way, God will answer. Who knows perhaps your "suddenly" is right around the corner?

For I am about to do something new. See, I have already begun! Do you not see it? I will make a pathway through the wilderness. I will create rivers in the dry wasteland (Isaiah 43:19 NLT).

It's Time to Start Dreaming Again!

We are God's masterpiece. Every part of us has been intricately woven together for a specific purpose by a skilled artisan. We may not understand our complexities and idiosyncrasies, but they were specifically designed by God to give him glory.

I don't know about you, but most times I don't feel, look, or act like a masterpiece. Most times, I'm a hot mess. I'm impulsive; speak when I shouldn't, overreact at times . . . yet in God's eyes, I'm a masterpiece, an integral part of a tapestry that only he sees. According to his Word there is a job only I can do. A purpose only I can fulfill. So amazing!

God wants to use every part of you, your victories, failures, weaknesses, and strengths. Nothing is wasted with him. Our suffering does not have to be in vain. Are you willing to give him everything? The future he has for you is better than you can imagine, and you will never know until you release yourself to him. Your Creator designed you with a specific purpose. Allow him to mold you and use your life for his glory. Then and only then will you live life to your greatest potential.

Story of Esther

Esther was a Hebrew orphan. In society's eyes, that was her identity. However, that was not her identity in God's eyes. He had something in store for her that would surpass her greatest imagination. In God's eyes she was a queen . . . not just any queen, but the very person God would use to save his people.

I'm sure there were times in her life when she felt ill-equipped for the task. If she maintained the title society placed on her, she would not have been able to stand up when it was needed. She would have continued in a state of insecurity wondering, "Why would anyone listen to me?" She would have lived in defeat and her people would have perished. Instead of allowing society to dictate who she should be, she willingly surrendered to God's leading. As a result, God used her in a supernatural way, beyond her human capacity, and brought deliverance and blessing to her people.

What about you? Where are you stuck in the mud of disillusionment depression, or hopelessness? What lies about yourself have you believed? The time has come to step on the obstacles that have kept you in a rut and get out of that ditch. God promises you a good future and hope. Grab hold of this promise and refuse to let your past dictate your future. You have a new identity.

Throughout scripture there are various instances when God changes someone's name: Abram to Abraham, Sarai to Sarah, Jacob to Israel, Simon to Peter, Saul to Paul. God transformed these individuals and set them on a new life changing course. The Lord gave them a whole new identity and called them to live a different life.

Today, receive the new name your heavenly Father bestows on you: CHOSEN. No more are you to identify as someone who has been rejected. You are to accept the identity Christ has given you.

The Lord has saved us, forgiven us, and bestowed a new identity to us, so that despite the brokenness of our past we can walk into a new life of healing and hope. By grace we leave behind the days of weeping and despair. We dream according to the inspiration of the Word and by faith we bear our new name in Christ. We trust his timing and move ahead because we are the beloved children of God. All glory to him.

Christ gives us a new name:
CHOSEN—CHILD OF THE ONE TRUE KING.

CHAPTER FOURTEEN: NEW IDENTITY

Prayer

Lord, I pray for a fresh vision for my future. I know you have a good future and a good hope for me (Jeremiah 29:11). Thank you for believing in me when no one else did. Help me to see myself through your eyes. I want to live a life worthy of your call (Ephesians 4:11). Knowing your love for me is limitless and unconditional, I pray you guide my steps as I enter a new chapter in my life. May I be fruitful in every good work (Colossians 1:9–10). You are the redeemer of my past, present and future. I trust you as my Lord and Savior and choose to follow you all the days of my life. In Jesus' name, Amen.

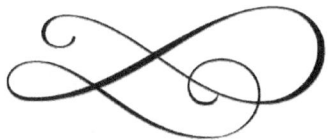

"Praise the Lord. Blessed are those who fear the Lord, who find great delight in his commands. Their children will be mighty in the land; the generation of the upright will be blessed. Wealth and riches are in their houses, and their righteousness endures forever. Even in darkness light dawns for the upright, for those who are gracious and compassionate and righteous. Good will come to those who are generous and lend freely, who conduct their affairs with justice. Surely the righteous will never be shaken; they will be remembered forever. They will have no fear of bad news; their hearts are steadfast, trusting in the Lord. Their hearts are secure, they will have no fear; in the end they will look in triumph on their foes. They have freely scattered their gifts to the poor, their righteousness endures forever; their horn will be lifted high in honor."

—Psalm 112:1–9

Reflection

Before answering these questions, ask the Holy Spirit to bring to mind the areas of your life addressed in this chapter which need healing and change.

1.   Where in your life do you feel stuck? How has your situation defined you? What part of your life seems dark and without hope?

2.   What dreams seem beyond your grasp? Describe them in detail and break them down in steps. Study them and make goals for yourself.

CONCLUSION

The first step in allowing God to begin the healing work in your heart is to accept the free gift of salvation given to us by the death and resurrection of Jesus Christ. On the cross Jesus took upon himself our sins, failures, disease, and judgements.

Your new beginning is a prayer away. If you have never done so, please pray the following prayer:

Dear Lord Jesus, I know that I am sinner and I ask for your forgiveness. I believe you died for my sins and rose from the dead. I turn from my sins and invite you to come into my heart and life. I choose today to trust and follow you as my Lord and Savior. In your name, I pray. Amen.

If you prayed this prayer for the first time, wanting to accept Christ as your Lord and Savior, congratulations! You are now a part of the family of God. Three things happen when you accept Christ:

1. You are forgiven of all of your sins (Romans 8, I John 1:9).

2. Your name is written in the Book of Life and now you have access to heaven for eternity (Romans 5:8, Revelations 3:5, Philippians 4:3).

3. The Holy Spirit comes to live inside of you. The Holy Spirit also known as the Comforter will guide and teach you in this new life (John 15:26, John 16:7–15, Ephesians 1:13–14).

It is important that you continue to read your Bible and get connected to a church that teaches sound Biblical doctrine that Jesus Christ is Lord and salvation comes only through him. God bless you on your new journey. I am excited for you and know God has a new beginning for you. I wish you many blessings!

ACKNOWLEDGMENTS

*T*he *Name Changer* has been a labor of love; love for God and for the countless people who have suffered because of divorce. I could not have completed this project without the help, prayer, and support of so many.

First, I would like to thank each of the women who courageously provided their testimonies. Thank you for your transparency and for allowing God to use your pain for his glory.

I would also like to thank all those who took the time to proof edit my manuscripts from inception to completion.

There are two women in particular who have been instrumental in making the dream of this book a reality. First, Jannis Powell, my editor, friend, cheerleader, and confidant. Thank you for never giving up on me. You are a bright light in this dark world. I appreciate your feedback, corrections, and additions. You are absolutely amazing!

Next, Melinda Martin, my publishing consultant and book designer. Thank you for your patience and endurance despite my indecisiveness and pickiness. You are highly gifted and made a difficult process joyful.

The Name Changer could not have been written without the love and support of my precious husband Trey; God has given me one of his greatest blessings in you.

To my precious children, Carisia, Cassandra, and Joshua—thank you for being so amazing and persevering with me through all of our ups and downs. I am blessed to be your mother and could not be prouder of you.

To Leah and Saige, you will forever be in my heart. I love you.

Cary Seaholm

Cary is a licensed clinical social worker, a former Florida Supreme Court certified family mediator and has developed parenting classes to aid those involved in child custody disputes. She has spent most of her career working with individuals and families in various clinical and professional settings.

Cary's personal and professional background provides her with both clinical and biblical insights to reach the root causes of pain and despair. As a therapist and professional speaker, her greatest desire is to see others transformed by God's love and to help women know and fully understand their identity in Christ.

Cary is a dedicated wife, loving mother of three, and a devoted Christian. She believes God can turn our biggest disappointments into our greatest testimonies for his glory.

Connect with the Author

www.chosencounseling.com

Facebook   @chosencounseling

Instagram   @chosencounseling